TOO DEEP FOR TEARS

*A Christian
response to
personal loss*

DOUGLAS
AND
ANN HARE

Copyright © 1995 by Douglas and Ann Hare

First published in 1995

ISBN 1-873796-57-9

Published by
Autumn House
Alma Park, Grantham, Lincolnshire
NG31 9SL, England

TOO DEEP FOR TEARS

DEDICATION

This book is written
with profound love
for David, Michael and Margaret;

with heartfelt thankfulness
for Catherine, Carolyn and Christopher;

with deep gratitude
for family and friends;

but especially it is
FOR JAMES

ACKNOWLEDGEMENTS

Much labour is required to bring a book to birth; but many were the helping hands we received. Initially there was a miscarriage (so to speak) when the original manuscript was in a bag stolen from our car and never recovered. We are grateful to Bishop Richard Third who readily assented to a three-month sabbatical which enabled us to start writing all over again. Many thanks, too, to those who laboured at the typing: Audrey Leede, Jan Gilliland, Ann Whitehead, and Joan Whitehead, for all of whom it was a service of love. Others provided oases of quiet for creative writing, and we wish to express our deep gratitude to John and Maureen Riley at Stanton House near Oxford; to John and Rita Jacobs for their lovely hideaway in the New Forest; to Bernard and Rosemary Johnson for the use of their home on the Gower. Writing a book in the midst of a busy ministry means a dependence on the support of others, and we are so grateful to all those who have so willingly provided this support. We have been encouraged to persevere, too, by Rosemary Attlee, by Noel Fellowes, and especially by Bridget and Adrian Plass, to whom we are most indebted for the Foreword. Our family acted as monitors by constantly checking progress, and by commenting on accuracy of fact or interpretation.

But the midwife-in-charge (to continue the metaphor) is our editor, David Marshall, so ably assisted by his wife Anita and all the team at Autumn House. We are most grateful to them for all the skilful help we have received.

Yet all life is God-given, and we acknowledge that He has prompted us to bring this book into the light of day. For our part we pray that just as our faith was strengthened through our devastating experiences, so this record may strengthen the faith of all who read it, and bring honour and glory to the God and Father of our Lord Jesus Christ.

The authors are willing to be contacted c/o the Publishers.

FOREWORD

Douglas and Ann Hare are unusual people, in the sense that they really do try to live out the Christian faith that lies at the very centre of their lives. I don't mean that they succeed all the time — they'd hate me to suggest that — but the desire genuinely to serve God and their neighbour constantly moulds and informs the shape and quality of their response to the world. I feel so fortunate to be able to count them among the friends that I would trust with fragile elements of my own personality.

I first met Douglas and Ann when I went to speak at their church in Margate some years ago. After the meeting I returned to their house to stay the night, and it was in the course of that evening that I heard about the comparatively recent death of their beloved son Mike in a road accident. I know that it's common to speak well of the dead, but it was clear that their assessment of Mike's fine qualities was not just the product of parental bias. The world had lost a fine young man, for reasons that lay hidden behind thick clouds of sorrow and loss, if they existed at all.

That evening I found myself wanting to weep in sympathy as waves of grief filled the sitting-room of the house where Mike had grown up. I had encountered grief before, of course, but never a grief so free of self-pity. Douglas and Ann were experiencing terrible hurt, but they were just as concerned about the hurt that had been caused by Mike's death in the lives of others. Furthermore, unlike many Christians, they were aware that the cross is an inescapable aspect of the long journey that takes us back to our Father in heaven. Like the good soldiers they are, they were prepared to include the weight of loss in the burden that their Master had commanded them to carry, and to continue to walk with Him in total trust.

These words are easy to write, but for the Hares, as for so many who are bereaved, the achievement of a proper equilibrium was not. The process goes on and on. This book is their account of the journey from sudden, heartbreaking sorrow, to the place where pain and peace lie down together, like the lion and the lamb. I know that many people will be helped and inspired by this story.

I urge you, as you read it, to be conscious that the words flow from good hearts. *ADRIAN PLASS*

MICHAEL　　　DOUGLAS　　　ANN　　　DAVID
CATHERINE　　　　MAGGIE　　　CAROLYN

The complete family.

TOO DEEP FOR TEARS

CONTENTS

SECTION ONE

DAVID'S STORY

Coming to terms with
a serious Accident

I

The long, exhausting autumn term was nearly over. It had begun months back in early September, with new classes, new pupils, new staff, and had trundled along fairly smoothly each day-by-demanding day. Now, in mid-December, it was almost over. I drove home wearily in the early evening darkness, slowing down as an ambulance sirened and flashed its way towards me, heading for the hospital. I thought momentarily of the occupant, then switched to home. It would be good to relax with the family for the next three weeks, enjoying Christmas together and putting school, with all its duties and responsibilities, behind me.

I taught at a boys' preparatory school, the junior department of a fair-sized public school. Half of our pupils were boarders, and this meant evening and weekend duties. We'd had something of a traumatic time recently, and the former headmaster had left at the end of the summer term. The new man was not coming until January, so the second master had run the school this term as acting head, and I was his deputy. It had been a good term, and there'd been a good spirit among the staff as we all pulled together. But we were tired, very tired. Tomorrow evening we'd all be assembling, with spouses, at our house for a buffet supper as a 'thank you' to John Dixon, the acting head, for his leadership, and to present him with a salver as a mark of our appreciation. Before that, I had just twenty-four hours to enjoy my family at our comfortable home.

We were a close-knit family, enjoying each other's company. My wife Ann was a good home-maker, exuding hospitality, relating easily to people in her bright and cheerful way. Our eldest son, David, 20, was in his second year at Reading University, reading agriculture. We were expecting him home this evening on his motor bike. Our second boy, Michael, had just finished at his boarding school near Bath, and was awaiting the results of his Oxbridge exams. Margaret, our youngest, was at the local grammar school, and had just started in the sixth form. Ann and I were committed Christians and each of our three youngsters had, independently, in their own way and in their own time and without pressure from us, committed their lives to Christ. This was a great unifying bond in our family as we all acknowledged an allegiance both to each other and to our Lord.

One blemish on the happy family face was a relationship that David had developed with a woman eleven years his senior. Six months previously, when he was 19 and she was 30, he'd told us that they were engaged; yet it was never made public within either family, as would usually be our custom. The difference in age, while not exactly immaterial, did not worry us unduly; the difference in temperament did. They were so wrapped up in each other that they did not seem to notice. But essentially it was a spiritual matter. Christians are people who have asked Jesus Christ to run their lives, so they are no longer self-centred but Christ-centred. Now while Maureen (as we'll call her) was, like David, a Christian, our spiritual antennae told us that this was a mismatch. We were unhappy about it — and so were many of our friends. This alliance of David's put an uneasy strain on his relationship not only with us, but also with his brother and sister. It isolated him from us all. He felt it, and we were aware of it.

It was good to be home. Ann was busy preparing the evening meal, the younger two were occupying themselves upstairs in their own rooms, and we were awaiting David's return before eating. The early evening news started on television and Ann went into the dining-room to watch it.

When the front door bell rang I answered it, and was surprised to find two policemen there.

'Mr Hare?' said the taller one.

'Yes,' I replied.

'Do you have a son, David?' he asked gently.

'Yes,' I replied again. What's he done? I wondered. Left his motor bike parked near the motorway approach road again?

'Do you mind if we come inside a moment, sir?' the officer broke in on my thoughts.

'Of course not,' I answered, and led them into the sitting-room.

Once seated, the officer began his story.

'I'm afraid I have to tell you that David has been knocked off his motor bike. He was found lying on the grass verge at Brooks End, near Birchington. A doctor has seen him, and an ambulance has taken him to Margate Hospital about fifteen minutes ago.' (The ambulance I met, I thought!) 'We don't know how badly he's injured, but he's being seen at the hospital now. I'm sorry to have to tell you all this.'

'Well, yes, thank you,' I said incongruously, courtesy covering my confusion.

'It doesn't seem as if there was another vehicle involved, or if there was, it didn't stop. Both the rider and bike were found by the driver of a following car. He stopped and phoned for the ambulance from a nearby garage. It came pretty quickly. A passing doctor then stopped and examined him before the ambulance took him to the casualty department.'

I was trying to take this all in. 'You say a doctor's seen him?' I was looking for reassurance while my heart was pounding with anxiety.

'That's right, sir, but we still don't know how badly he's injured.'

'I see,' I said, still bewildered. The policemen stood up. The other one now remembered something.

'The motor bike,' he said, 'was taken to the garage nearby — Brooks End Garage. You could collect it from there.'

'Yes, all right,' I replied. I was very tired and my reactions were slow.

'Sorry to have to bring bad news,' said the first policeman again.

'It can't be easy,' I replied as we moved into the hall.

He stopped and looked at me squarely. 'However often you have to do it, it never becomes easy.' He said.

I expressed my appreciation as I saw them out. Now to tell Ann, immersed in the national news, unaware of the dramatic domestic news. I took a deep breath and went into the dining-room.

'Ann, dear,' I said gently, 'the police have just been. It's David. He's been knocked off his motor bike and taken to Margate hospital. But a doctor's seen him.'

Ann sprang into action, walking swiftly into the hall and grabbing her coat. 'Come on,' she cried, 'we're going to the hospital now. We must find out how badly injured he is.'

As she reached the front door, she called upstairs to Mike.

'Mike, David's been badly hurt in an accident. We're going to Margate hospital to see him. Phone John Went and Donald Lugg (two local ministers) to tell them to PRAY!'

We set off on our short journey, while I filled Ann in with the details I knew.

As we hurried into casualty we asked a passing nurse where we'd find David.

'He's in there,' she said, nodding towards double doors, 'but you can't go . . . '

But Ann was already pushing the door open. There, ahead of us on a trolley lay David, naked, lying motionless on his stomach. There was hardly a bruise or a scratch on his body, but his face was turned away from us. His clothes, which had been cut from his body, were lying in a heap on the floor. All this we took in in a couple of seconds.

'You're not allowed in here,' said a nurse firmly.

'I'm his mother,' said Ann, equally firmly, adding, 'And I'm a nurse.'

'Maybe, but you're not allowed in here. He's about to be examined by a doctor.'

'Let me just see his face,' said Ann, stepping forward to look.

'You must leave,' repeated the nurse. 'At once!'

We retreated, but Ann had seen what she wanted to see. We were shown into a waiting-room, and sat down heavily.

'His body seems to be all right,' said Ann softly to me, 'but, oh, his face! It's swollen and puffy, his eye is closed fast, his mouth swollen up. He's blue with bruises. He's obviously still unconscious.' She paused, reflecting.

'I wonder,' she said, half to herself.

'Wonder what?'

'I wonder how long it was between the accident and the doctor treating him.'

'Why?' I asked.

'Because if he stopped breathing, as he probably did, if it lasted for any time he would suffer from permanent brain damage,' she explained patiently.

'What would that mean?'

'It would mean, Douglas darling, that he would be left a cabbage, unable to move his body — even unable to speak. I don't think I could face that.'

'Neither could I,' I added.

We retreated into our own thoughts, sending up arrow-prayers for David and for the doctors treating him. Inevitably my thinking drifted to imagining my fine, upright, athletic son as a human cabbage, imprisoned in an immobile, inactive frame. I knew I couldn't face it. I'm not sure that David could, either; wouldn't *actual* death be preferable to a living death?

I shared these thoughts with Ann, and discovered that she was thinking the same, wrestling with the possible prospect of a son unable to communicate, confined to a wheelchair for the rest of his waking life. I'd already decided, and given up the struggle.

'Lord,' I prayed silently, 'lay your healing hand upon David, I pray. But, Lord, if he's only going to be a human cabbage, I pray that you will take him and give us the courage to face his loss.' It was a feeble prayer, but I meant it, every word.

I never thought that I would ever pray for my own son's

death. Should I have done so? Was it morally right? I remembered an incident when as a small boy I discovered a young bird with both wings broken, flapping about in the garden, weak with pain and exhaustion. 'Mummy,' I called out to the kitchen, 'there's a bird here with both wings broken. What can we do for it?' My mother came out into the garden to look. 'It's best to kill it, dear, and put it out of its agony,' she said softly. She spoke so tenderly I knew it was right, and didn't argue. I just went and fetched a brick and dropped it on its head; then I dug a shallow grave and buried the body. 'Poor bird,' I said quietly, 'but you're out of your misery now.'

Since then I've always believed there's more to life than being alive; that life does not equal existing, just breathing. But who is to say that life should no longer exist in each individual case? Who is to 'play God'? That's often the doctor's dilemma; sometimes a close relative's decision. But I left it to God: 'Please take him, rather than just keep him alive for an existence.' Yet I could only say this as a Christian, knowing that Dave was a Christian who had embraced eternal life in Christ.

At last a doctor came and sought us out. He was an Indian with a gentle manner.

'It is difficult to say how serious the injury to your son is,' he told us. 'He has a fractured skull, and is paralysed down the right sight. His head and face are very bruised, and he is still unconscious.'

These were the facts. What we wanted to know was the prognosis.

'Will he recover?' Ann asked.

The doctor hesitated, searching her eyes.

'It's all right,' Ann said, 'we'd rather know now, and be prepared. Do you think he'll recover?'

'It's difficult to say,' he repeated. 'I just don't know at this stage.'

'Can we see him?' Ann persisted.

Again he hesitated.

'I am a nurse,' Ann went on.

'All right,' he replied, 'just briefly. He's in the ICU, of course. Speak to the nurse in charge there.'

We thanked him and he left us as we made our way to the Intensive Care Unit. We knocked and a male nurse came out. Ann recognized him as someone she'd once worked with. When we asked if we could see David he hesitated, and Ann pressed him to let us in.

'All right,' he said. 'But I warn you, his face is an ugly mess.'

The room was dimly lit, and David, flat on his back, was the sole occupant. Tubes protruded from his body to different places, and a cardiograph machine bleeped his heartbeats. His breathing was slow but regular, and he was quite obviously in a coma. The charge nurse was right: his face was an ugly mess. His left eye was closed and very swollen, his lips like sausages, his nose flattened like a boxer's. But there were only a couple of small scars on his forehead and upper lip; no open wounds or blood. Apart from the puffiness, he looked very peaceful. Ann and I just gazed upon him silently, but fervently praying in our hearts.

A houseman appeared and we were ushered outside. At the entrance to a ward we slumped into the chairs provided. A nurse came and offered us tea, that great British reviver for any and every occasion. It wasn't how we liked it, but we drank it down gratefully.

The houseman reappeared but said nothing to us. We were allowed back in again, and talked to the charge nurse.

'Has a consultant seen him yet?' Ann asked.

'The duty consultant is in Folkestone, but we can't get hold of him at the moment.'

Folkestone, I thought, that's over an hour's drive away!

Ann and I each took hold of David's limp hands, and again prayed for our dearly-beloved son: for fullness of life, or for fullness of death — but not for in-between.

'We ought to contact Mike and Maggie,' said Ann, ever practical. 'There's a pay-phone in the entrance hall.'

'I'll go and phone them,' I replied, glad just to be able to do something. Waiting seemed so wasteful and made me feel so helpless.

I phoned the others, explaining that we had no idea when we'd be back. Mike said he'd phoned John and Donald, and that Donald would be round at the hospital later. People had been mobilized to pray.

I rejoined Ann, now seated outside the ICU.

'I've been thinking,' she said, softly but firmly. 'David should be seen by a specialist. If the duty consultant isn't going to see him, is there anyone else? Well, there are two consultants I've worked with who've always said to us nurses, "If you or your family ever need us professionally, we'll always be available to you." Do you think I should call one of them?'

Medical etiquette and professional practice always left me quite bewildered. I didn't know the 'correct' answer, though I was quite sure of the obvious, practical one. But Ann had been trained in a strict school at a London teaching hospital where the lines had been firmly drawn.

'If they offered, why not accept?' I asked pragmatically.

'Perhaps,' said Ann, still with lingering doubts. Then the thought of her ailing son took over, and her resolve hardened. 'Yes,' she said finally, 'I will! Now, which one? I think I find Mr Klugman the easier of the two. Shall I try to contact him?'

'I should,' I encouraged her.

She'd made her decision and acted upon it. First she spoke to the ICU charge nurse, thanking him for all he was doing. He was as concerned as anyone to have his patient seen by a consultant.

'Would you mind,' she asked, 'if I contacted Mr Klugman? Only, he offered to see any of my family if we ever needed his care.'

'Go ahead,' he replied. 'Use the phone here.'

She went down to the reception. In five minutes she was back with a slight smile of triumph on her strained face.

'He's in the hospital!' she said eagerly, 'living in a flat while he moves house. He's coming round here in two minutes.'

He came and Ann greeted him. 'This is very good of you, . . . '

'I'm only too glad to help,' he cut her short. 'I just hope I can be of some use.'

As we shook hands I liked the look of the man: a strong aquiline face with penetrating, smiling eyes, a thoughtful forehead topped with black curly hair. 'There's not much that misses him,' I surmised, 'no one's going to pull the wool over those eyes. And I expect he's blunt and straight-talking with others, too!'

He went into the ICU and I shared my impressions with Ann, who confirmed them. Ten minutes later he emerged. As I expected, his words were direct.

'He's had a serious head injury which has left him para-lysed down the right side. I've examined him thoroughly, but there's a lot of bruising to the head. It's too early to say yet if he'll recover, and if so, to what extent. But he's young and very fit and healthy, and this is a plus which will work in his favour. But at the moment I can't say.'

Ann probed. 'What do you think his chances are?'

He looked at her squarely but kindly, and hesitated before answering. 'It really is hard to say. About fifty-fifty, I should think.'

We shook hands and thanked him for his time and trouble.

'I must go now, but I'll come and see him tomorrow.'

'Fifty-fifty,' I kept thinking. A 50 per cent chance of David living. Even so, there was no knowing to what extent he'd be handicapped or crippled. I suddenly felt very, very tired.

A nurse noticed and offered us more tea, for which we were most grateful. We were determined to stay on hand for

David, in case he recovered consciousness, but we could take the vigil in turns. It was nine o'clock. I would go home and sleep for five hours, then come and relieve Ann, who'd then catch up on her sleep. One of us would always be with David.

Donald Lugg breezed in; big, burly, bearded Donald usually had a jovial manner which on occasions could be a little overbearing. Now he was tenderness itself, gentle and compassionate. He put his large arms on each of our shoulders, and prayed fervently for us and for David. For a time David had worshipped at his church, and we all had a strong rapport. We went into the ICU and Donald laid hands on David, praying earnestly for him. David lay still, quite motionless apart from his slow, regular deep breathing. Ann found a chair and sat by David's bedside. Encouraged by the nurse, she took his hand and talked to him, recalling people and events familiar to him, trying to penetrate the dark haze around his mind and reach his consciousness. We knew it was going to be a long, hard struggle.

Donald left, and we felt better for his visit as his genuineness and sincerity shone through. I left soon after; we had two other children at home who needed me. I was exhausted, and found the whole situation at the hospital almost unbearable.

Once home I suddenly remembered the staff party due to take place at our house the next evening. I phoned a colleague, explained what had happened, and asked him to ring round the others, saying that the party was cancelled. He willingly agreed, and I felt relieved.

I spent an hour or so with the youngsters, but I couldn't settle. My mind was focused on that still figure in intensive care. Mike and Margaret did have each other, so after a while I wished them a good night's sleep and rushed back to the hospital. There was no change. David, with Ann at his bedside, was just as I'd left him. But we were both exhausted, drained of all energy. We decided to make use of the hospital quiet room, taking it in turns to doze in an easy chair there, one resting, one watching with David. So we passed the night.

The next day Ann went home at 7am to see the youngsters and have breakfast with them. She was back at the hospital at 9am, when I drove home for food and creature comforts. What a blessing, I thought, that he's at the local hospital and not somewhere miles away. Maggie offered to get the lunch, and mid-morning I rejoined Ann. She told me that Norman Baldock, the vicar of Margate and chaplain to the hospital, had been in and anointed David with oil as he had prayed for his healing.

Mr Klugman had also been in, true to his word. He had examined David again, and then given Ann an agonizingly difficult choice.

'I have a bed at the Brook Hospital,' he had said, 'where they are very skilled in dealing with head injuries. But the Brook is at Woolwich, and that means a long journey in an ambulance which at this stage could be detrimental. However, I could send him there if you'd like me to.'

Ann spoke to the consultant. 'What do you recommend?' she said.

'They're doing all they can for him here,' he replied. 'I don't think there's anything more that could be done.'

'And the journey to Woolwich could well be harmful?' Ann needed reassuring.

'Yes, it could.'

In the end, we decided that if Mr Klugman was happy with the care David was receiving at Margate then so were we. We chose to leave him where he was for the time being, but to keep the option open.

The vigil continued. We were known now to the ICU staff, who allowed us to be at David's bedside most of the time. But there was no change in his condition, no change at all. One of the nurses asked us casually if he liked music. We smiled. David was the most unmusical in our family, usually singing flat and out of tune. We asked her why she'd asked. She replied that sometimes constant playing of familiar themes, something they would remember or respond to, can get through to a person in a coma.

'I know!' I jumped up excitedly. 'Cricket! David is mad on cricket, and there's a test series on now in Australia. If we brought a small radio in, we could play the ball-by-ball commentary!'

This was agreed, and I brought in a portable radio and set it up for him to hear the cricket commentary in the hope that it might break through into his consciousness.

The long day dragged on. The strain was telling now. We were on edge and jumpy. We'd been tired enough before this happened, and with all the stress, plus only a few hours of snatched sleep, we were both quite exhausted. By seven o'clock, with no change in Dave, we realized we were all in. We decided we'd both spend the night at home, hopefully get a good night's rest, and so be able to resume our watch in a more alert state the next day. We informed the nurse of our decision, gave her our telephone number, and returned home to bed, to sleep, sleep, sleep.

After driving the young people up to the early morning family service at church next morning, we returned to the hospital. David was much the same. We turned on the test match commentary from 'down-under', which at least diverted my thoughts; yet despite my passion for the game, I couldn't take a lot of interest then. It was all too remote, so unreal. The only reality for me was my son, lying stretched out on a hospital bed in a coma, with only a fifty-fifty chance of surviving. Even cricket, one of the great joys of my life, was like ashes in my mouth.

We sat and watched and waited. The male nurse who'd been on duty on the Friday evening came back on. He looked at us seriously.

'You must realize,' he said, 'that when patients come out of a prolonged coma it can be very unpleasant, very unpleasant indeed.' Ann nodded, but I looked mystified. Surely this was what we were all waiting for.

'You see,' he went on, 'they don't know where they are. They can't relate to reality. So they become violent, obstreperous, shouting — even ranting and raving. Sometimes we have to hold them down. It's not at all pleasant.'

I looked at my motionless son with all the tubes coming out of his body, and his heart monitored on the cardiograph behind him. I decided I'd rather he was active and shouting than passive and silent.

That evening phone calls of concern from church people kept coming; also there were invitations to lunch for the next three days, which was a marvellous practical help.

Later that night, while praying for my son, I had a clear 'word' from the Lord. It was not an audible voice, but an inner conviction, yet just as real. I'd been praying for David's full healing, but also that the Lord would take him rather than leave him helplessly alive with an active mind trapped inside a lifeless body, unable to express itself. Resonant as a chime, the conviction came to me in the words of Scripture: '"This sickness will not end in death. No, it is for God's glory, so that God's Son my be glorified through it."' (1 John 11:4.) From that moment onwards I never doubted that David would recover, and recover fully. It was the Lord's word to me, and I believed it and trusted it implicitly.

I shared this conviction with Ann. Her medical knowledge made it more difficult for her to accept. She was struggling with all the possibilities: praying for full healing for David, but now able to say, albeit very reluctantly, 'Give me the grace to accept the "whatever", and the strength to cope with a son in a wheelchair, and even a son who is a human cabbage, if that can give glory to you.' It was a courageous prayer, and one I'd not been able to pray; even so, she feared what she had prayed for.

What is prayer? Has it any point or use, or is it just a psychological safety-valve, for use at times of great personal stress or crisis, a feeling that we can call hopefully upon a higher power than our helpless selves? For the Christian, prayer is real and deep and meaningful, aligning them with God's will. Jesus taught us to pray 'Thy will be done', and all over the world millions upon millions say it every day, too often unaware of its true meaning. For it is not a fatalistic acceptance, a 'that's life' sort of attitude: whatever happens to me, good or ill, is God's will for me. Far from it. What it really means is that I want to be so open to God that His will may be done in my life. A Christian is one who is seeking to live for God's glory, not for his own self-interest. So for him or her, 'Thy will be done' means 'I want God to work in my life all that will bring glory to Him, not to me'. But the Christian is still a fallen creature, and still seeks 'the power and the glory' for himself. Hence our need to pray 'Thy will be done' every day — and to mean it.

There's a remarkably candid insight into this in John's gospel (12:27-30), where Jesus is shown to be caught in the dilemma of how to pray. '"Now my heart is troubled",' he says, '"and what shall I say? 'Father, save me from this hour'?"' That's how *we* instinctively pray, especially when our 'heart is troubled', in times of crisis or upset, of distress or fear: 'Father, save me; Father, help me; O God, get me out of this mess!' The object of our prayer is always ME — self. Jesus poses this as a question: Should I say 'Father, save me from this hour'? He then answers His own question with a resounding 'No', and prays the only true prayer: '"Father, glorify your name!"' The object is now God's glory — whatever! And for Jesus 'whatever' meant the cross — and He knew it! Yet as soon as He prayed this prayer, it was audibly answered: '"I have glorified it, and will glorify it again."' The crowd that was there, we are told, 'said it had thundered; others said an angel had spoken to him.' But Jesus knew, and said, '"This voice was for your benefit, not mine."' So should it not teach us that our prayers must ever be for God's glory? 'For *thine* is the kingdom, the power, and the glory, for ever and ever, Amen.'

On Monday, as we entered the ICU after lunch there was

someone standing, staring out of the window. It was Maureen, David's girl-friend. She didn't turn round when we came in, but stood looking out into the void. We sensed, too, the void in her life, which David's friendship had managed to fill. Ann greeted her: 'Hello, Maureen!' and went over to kiss her. But she wasn't given the opportunity. Maureen simply turned and stared down at David, making little effort to acknowledge us, let alone relate to us. It was a situation that saddened us greatly and added to the strain.

The days dragged by with barely perceptible improvements in David. The swelling on his face slowly began to go down. He moved his leg slightly on his right side. The heartbeats, though slow, were still regular. We continued our vigil and prayers: we lived in faith and in hope.

About the middle of the week, just five days before Christmas, Maggie suddenly said: 'Aren't we going to have a Christmas this year, then?'

'Yes, darling, of course we are,' Ann replied, 'why do you ask?'

'Well, we haven't got a tree.'

We felt rebuked; so absorbed were we with our sick son that we'd neglected our healthy children, and forgotten about Christmas. So on the way back from hospital that lunchtime, we stopped and bought a Christmas tree, the finest we could afford. It was soon potted, and Mike and Maggie spent the afternoon decorating it. Somehow it restored our spirits a little.

The luncheon invitations kept coming. Without once inviting ourselves out, we were provided with a hot meal for twelve consecutive days, which meant that Ann hardly needed to think about food or cooking. Such a relief!

But I had something else to think about: David's motor bike. The policeman had said it had been left at a nearby garage. I traced them in the telephone directory and rang them. A rather abrasive man answered, saying that he wanted the bike removed from his forecourt, and reminding me curtly that there'd be a parking fee to pay. I told him I'd come and collect it as soon as I could make arrangements.

'How sad,' I reflected, 'how very sad that some people can't lend a helping hand, can't do something for nothing, and even have to exploit other people's misfortunes.'

I telephoned the motor cycle repair shop and authorized them to collect it, and then to repair and sell it. One thing we had firmly decided was that David would never ride a motor bike again. Phoning back to the garage to instruct them to release the bike, I got a lady this time.

'All right,' she said, 'I'll hand the bike over to them — and there'll be no charge for parking it. How is the young man?' I told her he was still unconscious, but we believed he'd pull through.

The daily vigil continued, though we both came home for the nights now: we needed the rest, the great restorative. But we'd left our phone number in the Unit, in case they needed to contact us.

Sunday was Christmas Eve. What an eerie Christmas this would be: little place this year for family fun, feasting, or festivities. Yet we all believed in God, and loved the Lord Jesus, and wanted to celebrate His coming into the world. Could we, with hearts so heavy with apprehension? Yes, we could and should, for God was the reality at the centre of our lives, the source of moral strength and spiritual peace. Abandon Him and we might as well have given up on David, on life itself. So we made time to worship, and we made arrangements to take Communion.

Early that evening we were surprised, but grateful, to have a visit from my sister and brother-in-law. They'd come from North-west London, where Derek had a general practice as a doctor. He'd driven down with Audrey, my sister, both to comfort us and to see David for himself. At the ICU he wanted to examine David personally, even if it meant trampling on medical etiquette. We waited outside the Unit with Audrey while he did so.

He emerged after about twenty minutes.

'He's not as bad as I thought he might be. Mind you, it's still pretty serious, and he's quite poorly, but there's no apparent reason why he shouldn't pull through. True, he's paralysed down the right side, but that should improve considerably. He's strong and fit, and his breathing is regular. I'm quite hopeful that he'll come through — but it will take time.'

We were encouraged by his comments, reinforcing as they did the opinion of Mr Klugman, confirming, too, our 'word from the Lord'.

We were grateful for their visit, travelling two and a half hours each way on a dark, wet Sunday evening in December, and Christmas Eve at that, just to reassure us about David. Family ties assume an important priority at times of domestic crises.

That evening we went to the midnight Communion service at our local church. We were conscious that many eyes were upon us, and many unspoken questions must have been directed at us. We were aware, too, of an empathy with us: 'If one part suffers, every part suffers with it.' We needed the spiritual strength of the Bread and Wine. We needed those strengthening words from the Prayer Book: 'Feed on Him in your heart by faith with thanksgiving.' That's just what we needed to do, day by wearying day. Only thus could we build up our inner resources, our moral fibre, our spiritual reserves of energy, by 'feeding on Him', by drawing that very special inner strength from Him. As the bread nourishes the body, so we believe the symbolic bread of Communion nourishes the soul.

Christmas Day: We worshipped with Mike and Maggie at family service in the morning and then dashed up to the hospital. We greeted the staff and gave each of them a little gift. At 12.30 Donald Lugg arrived with a portable Communion set. We invited the staff to join us, which they did, and so we took Holy Communion together in the Intensive Care Unit, and offered up prayers for David's healing and wholeness. It was a memorable and moving service, for when two or three are gathered in Christ's name, there is He in the midst of them: and we knew He was with us then.

Some friends had invited all four of us to join them for Christmas lunch. As well as their large family they had invited friends and neighbours, so about fifteen of us sat round the large table and enjoyed the traditional turkey and trimmings. The cheerfulness was not forced, the heartiness not hollow: for we all loved the Lord, and in his grace before the meal, our host committed David to God's care and keeping. On the basis of God's love for each one of us, of His watching over our loved ones, and of our fellowship together in His name, we could be truly cheerful, and rejoice.

But the meal over, we excused ourselves and hurried back to the hospital. David seemed to have stirred a little: he'd moved his good side again. Yet all the time I knew that not only would he survive, but recover. It wasn't a question of 'if', it was only a matter of how long it would take for him to be fully healed.

In addition to my God-given conviction that 'this sickness is not unto death' — which of course I'd shared with Ann — another Scripture was given to us. We'd managed to keep up with our daily Bible reading. We were using *Living Light* at the time, a collection of Scripture verses arranged for daily reading by themes. A verse which kept occurring, and stood out on stalks for both of us, was one we'd never noticed before. In addition, it would always seem to be one of the lessons if we went to a church service, or a text that someone would include in a letter. We knew it was for us, and we knew, too, that it referred to David:

'"I know the plans I have for you," declares the Lord, "plans to prosper you and not to harm you, plans to give you hope and a future."' (Jeremiah 29:11.)

We were both quite certain that God had a plan for David, a plan for his good, to give him a future and a hope. And that certainty gave us a serenity, an inner peace that passes all understanding. And that, for both Ann and me, was our best Christmas gift that dark December in 1978.

II

There was some improvement apparent in David's condition. His eye was now open, his face less puffy, his lips more normal. There was also some movement in his body. We believed that he may well have turned the corner, and was on the uphill climb to fuller life.

About the middle of the week after Christmas, David Klugman came to see David in the ICU, and gave him a thorough examination.

He emerged smiling. 'I should say he's pulling through,' he spoke warmly. 'There's still bruising in the brain, but it's subsiding. His general fitness has helped a lot. I think he'll regain some degree of mobility too, but I'm not promising anything at this stage. Don't expect a miracle, though! It'll take time, very probably a long time.'

'How long?' I asked. 'If he's not brain damaged, how long before he can go back to university?'

'Providing there's no damage to the brain,' the surgeon replied cautiously, 'it will be eighteen months at the earliest, more likely two years.'

My face fell; I had no idea it would be such a long haul. Our certainty that he would recover was now justified, but we didn't know to what extent he would recover, nor how long it would take. 'Don't expect miracles,' the specialist had said. 'Why not?' I thought; 'we worship a God of miracles! Did He not tell us that He had plans for David, "plans for good and not for evil, to give him a future and a hope"?' While we thanked God fervently in our hearts for David's improvement, progress and prognosis, we redoubled our prayers for a full and speedy recovery.

The consultant was talking to Ann. 'I think we could discharge him from intensive care soon and send him on to a ward; but not here. I'll arrange for him to go to the Royal Sea Bathing Hospital at Westbrook on Friday.' This was good news indeed; not only was David fit enough to go on to a ward, he was fit enough to travel to another hospital, one that was within walking distance of our home.

On the Friday I took Ann to Margate hospital. She was to escort David in the ambulance, while I drove back to the 'Sea Bathing' to await them. Although it was a positive step forward — David discharged from Intensive Care after two weeks — it was a difficult journey for Ann. For David was still in a coma, lying almost motionless on the stretcher. He seemed quite unaware of the move, showing no sign of recognition, just rolling his eyes upward. Ann was nearly choked, watching her well-built son lying there on his stretcher bed, making no response whatever.

The 186-year-old 'Sea Bathing' hospital was an elderly, dignified edifice, built at the end of the eighteenth century on the cliff-top overlooking the North Sea. Its large verandas (now glassed in) were for the tuberculosis patients of that era, providing lashings of healthy ozone and sea air. Ann had worked here as a staff nurse for some years and was well-known to the staff, including the sister of the ward to which David was being transferred.

The ambulance arrived and David was carried by stretcher to the ward where (though he didn't know it) he was treated royally. But, two weeks after his accident, he was still unconscious. His face was much clearer now, his features more pronounced. It could almost be said that he was beginning to look quite healthy, and quite noticeably the healing processes were working overtime in him. But he was still in a coma, and we still didn't know what condition he'd be in when he emerged from it. We simply trusted, and prayed, and clung to the promises of God.

That weekend, the last of the old year, I decided we'd better send out our annual Christmas cards and letters. They'd been ready to go a fortnight before, but the accident had forestalled all that. We decided to add a personal postscript. So I typed a card-sized piece, explaining that David had had a serious accident on 15 December and was still in a coma. I asked every recipient to pray briefly for him on Tuesday 9 January at 8pm when we would be holding a bedside service for him in the ward. I reproduced this note, sending off 120 of them with our belated Christmas cards and annual letter. If we were looking for a miracle we knew we had to mobilize the great spiritual force of prayer.

What is prayer for, and what does it do? Christians pray both because Jesus told them to, and because He set us a fine example of dedicated praying. 'Very early in the morning, while it was still dark, Jesus got up, left the house and went off to a solitary place, where he prayed.' (Mark 1:35.) Essentially, Christians pray to be in touch with God, whom they acknowledge as a loving Father. However, prayer is not trying to persuade God to do something for us, not attempting to get Him to change His mind, or His ways, to do something He's reluctant to do (though some prayers seem like that). Nor is it asking God to 'bless' what we've already decided to do (and many prayers are like that, especially at church meetings!). God wants us to pray and delights in our prayers, but what do they actually achieve?

There's a mystery here, as we seek to penetrate the spiritual realm. Archbishop William Temple once said: 'I've noticed that when I pray, "coincidences" happen!' Prayer is undoubtedly a great spiritual weapon, a powerful spiritual resource. My own belief is that prayer somehow releases some of God's spiritual energy into the world, into a situation, into a person's being. I believe that God has chosen to limit His almighty power to the ability of His people to pray, and when they pray that power is released. So when the prayer is focused or directed upon someone or something, God's energy will be thus focused and directed.

This has Scriptural warrant. When Jesus was in His home town of Nazareth, we are told that, 'He could not do any miracles there, because of their lack of faith'. In other words, the people's lack of faith (and prayer is *ipso facto* an act of faith) hindered Jesus' power to bestow spiritual and practical blessings. It's an awesome thought.

There seemed to be a little more animation in David's face that Sunday. We continued to chat constantly to him, though without evoking any response. Yet his eyes were brighter without showing any recognition. There was some movement in his body, too, and the nurses found a hospital gown and propped him up into a sitting position. He was more in control of his body it seemed; his head did not roll onto his neck and he was able to move his limbs slightly on his right side.

It was New Year's Eve that Sunday, and I went to church with Mike and Maggie for the evening service, leaving Ann at the hospital with Dave. It was an inspiring service of thanksgiving and praise, and of rededication of ourselves to God for His service in the coming year. On the way home we stopped at the hospital to collect Ann. Just as she was about to leave, impulsively she turned and leant over David's bed, saying, 'Give your old Mum a kiss!' as she bent down towards his face. Slowly he turned his head and his bruised lips brushed her cheek. We really whooped with joy and cried with delight. At last! At long last there'd been a breakthrough, a response! The New Year was going to be all right after all!

Eagerly we went to the hospital the next day. Yes, David was gradually regaining consciousness after two and a half weeks in a coma. The words of warning from our charge nurse came to mind: be prepared for him to be very disturbed. But all we wanted now was to see him animated, showing signs of life, comprehension and communication. We realized that we needed to bring others in, to involve him in communication, to try to break through the sound barrier, to enable him to relate to reality. So friends he knew, objects he was familiar with; this was what was needed to bring him back into our world.

It gradually dawned on us that his last awareness of consciousness was riding a motor bike towards his home on a dark December night, ten days before Christmas. Now he was in a totally unfamiliar hospital ward, pyjama-clad, with other patients, and strange people attending to his needs. It would be a small wonder if he did not have a sense of unreality, little surprise if he felt in a world apart as he slowly regained consciousness. A possible answer was to bring people from his previous known world into his present unfamiliar one.

So whenever his college friends phoned to ask after his condition, as they frequently did, we invited them to come and see him, to talk to him, to try to relate to him and break through the barrier. We also told them about the special service on 9 January, and of the focus of prayer at 8 pm that evening. These young people responded magnificently. They travelled to Margate singly, in twos and threes, just to spend an hour or two talking to Dave, usually with no response. But they persevered, and we marvelled at their generosity of time and spirit. Usually they declined our offer of overnight hospitality, but were grateful for a hot meal before returning home. Gradually, ever so gradually, David's awakening began and slowly developed.

If the first awareness had been on New Year's Eve, the first sign came on New Year's Day. The sister was anxious that he was lifted out of bed, to sit in an armchair next to it. However, the hospital gown was thin and his own was in Reading. He was cold, so Ann brought him in a couple of sweaters to choose from. She offered them both, and said gently, 'Which one would you like?' Slowly he lifted his arm and pointed to one of them. He'd heard, and he'd responded!

Now that there was an awakening to consciousness, other things developed. The nurses began to feed him solid food, which he slowly chewed and swallowed. There was still a glazed, uncomprehending look in his eyes, but we pinned our hopes on these responsive actions. A few days later the physiotherapists came and took a good look at him. There was now an urgent need to begin exercising the limbs and muscles down his right side to get them active again. Once more we were warned it would be a long, slow, uphill process.

There were many inquiries about David's health — by letter, phone and visit — especially since we'd sent out all those footnotes to our Christmas cards. Mike and Maggie were quite marvellous coping with these, easing this particular burden from our shoulders. If we were deeply moved by all the interest from friends and relations, we were profoundly touched by the concern of casual acquaintances. When the milkman came to collect his money each week he would ask 'how's the boy?' with total concern on his face. If I called in at the newsagent's for a paper I'd be asked, 'How's your son getting on?' Even in our individualistic society there is still a spirit of community abroad, an awareness of caring.

There was one lady who lived in a neighbouring street whom we'd smile at when taking our respective dogs for a walk. Passing our house one day with her Henry, a fierce-looking, though docile boxer, she saw Ann outside and stopped to ask after David. Then she told Ann, 'You know, I've been praying for your son. Before, whenever I've prayed, I've never really thought it got anywhere — my prayers just bounced off the walls. But this time I got through. I know I got through!' She smiled and went on her way with Henry, leaving Ann deeply touched — and humbled, too.

All this time Mike and Maggie had been a great strength to us. As concerned as they were about their brother, they soon realized that their role was back-up; helping to get meals, doing the household chores and walking the dog.

Now that David was in a public ward we were not strictly allowed to visit him in the mornings. There were tests, exercises and doctors' rounds, and we were best out of the way. So we had our mornings at home and began once more to pick up the varied ingredients of home life: cleaning, cooking, shopping, and so on. Maggie had just embarked on her 'A' level course, and soon her term would begin. Mike was now visiting the Job Centre — and also the Unemployment Exchange. Having left school he needed employment (even casual) before starting at university in the autumn. He'd applied to work at a Christian guest house in Israel in March for a few months and was waiting to hear about this. Also, he was awaiting apprehensively the results of his Oxbridge exams, which would decide his long-term future.

The weather was wintry cold now: there was snow on the road, and an icy wind blew through one's bones. Most nights and some days there was a keen frost, and this meant glassy or gritted roads in the morning.

Mike came home excitedly one day in early January. 'I've got a job!' he announced triumphantly.

'What is it — and where is it?' we enquired.

He laughed. 'It's at Manston Airport. They need someone to clean aeroplanes.'

His sister hooted: 'You!' she laughed. 'Mrs Mopp for an aeroplane. I can just see you in an apron and headscarf hoovering the carpets and seats! Have you got your dustpan and brush ready?'

'No, you Wally!' Mike retorted. 'I've got to clean the *outside* of these planes; get the snow off the wings and the ice off the glass; it's a man's job all right!'

Now Ann became concerned. 'Have you some warm clothing, dear? You'll need thick gloves, and a woolly hat, and a warm jacket, especially if you're outside all day.'

Mike as usual laughed away her fears. 'I'll be all right,' he said, reassuringly. 'Trouble is, they can't guarantee it as regular work. It depends on the weather, on the aircraft that are needed, and other factors as well. The pay isn't much cop, either. But it's a job, and we'll see how we get on.'

'How will you get there?' I asked.

'I'll go on my bike,' he replied jauntily.

'Not in this weather, Mike!' I said, quietly but firmly, thinking of David and the result of his being on two wheels in bad weather. 'When do you have to be there?'

'Seven o'clock, Dad; but don't worry, I'll be all right.'

'The roads to Manston are minor ones — they'll be

packed with snow, frozen over, treacherous for a bike. I'll take you each morning in the car.'

Mike capitulated, sensing how we felt. 'Thanks, Dad,' he said. 'We'll see how it goes.'

So each dark, icy morning I drove Mike out to Manston Airport. Sometimes we'd put his bike in the back of the estate car so that he could cycle home when his work was done; this could be midday or mid-afternoon, depending on the extent to which the aircraft were ice-bound. Mike himself usually came home ice-bound. It was chilling work with the bitter north winds sweeping straight from the North Sea across the flat airfield. But Mike never complained, and was his usual cheery self when he came home.

We still spent hours with David each day. We talked to him endlessly, but still there was no verbal response. He looked at us with uncomprehending eyes, so that we knew we hadn't penetrated his world.

Slowly and gradually there was more movement in David's body; but we realized he wasn't eating as he should be. The nurses were giving him his tray of food, but not feeding him; they just took the tray away untouched. So Ann arranged to go in each lunch-time, and spoon-fed him herself — a slow process. Yet it was the least we could do to help our son regain his strength.

There was the spiritual strength, too, that he needed, and we began to prepare for the service on Tuesday evening. Ann cleared it with the ward sister, then I arranged for John Went to come and give us an informal communion service around David's bedside.

Some of his friends from Reading University Christian Union had phoned to say they'd like to be present. One who could not come for the Tuesday came the weekend before instead, staying with us overnight; he spent much time with Dave — talking, encouraging, praying, seeking in every way to get through to the person inside the weakened body. We were very touched by his Christian devotion.

Tuesday evening came. About a dozen of us had gathered

at David's bedside by 8pm. David himself, freshly washed and brushed up, was seated in his gown in a large padded armchair beside the bed. He seemed more alert than we'd seen him, more aware of what was going on around him. John Went explained that we would give communion to each other, beginning at one end, and then offering the bread and wine to our neighbour, until the last person (who was Ann, standing next to David) would bring it back and give communion to John himself.

So we began our little bedside service, and Jesus' promise, 'Wherever two or three are gathered together in my name, there am I in the midst of them' was very real to each of us. We all had books, including David, to follow the order of service, but John had explained to me that he would abbreviate the full service. At one point he deliberately omitted an optional section, and a deep voice spoke up:

'You've missed some out!'

It was David! We were startled, amazed, delighted — all at once! He was actually following the service, reading it, comprehending it. Our cup of joy was filling up.

The service continued: we shared 'the peace' with each other and with David, we laid hands on him and prayed for him, we received the Bread and Wine together. After Ann had received, as last in the line, she walked round to give Communion to John Went. As she did so, a plaintive voice called out: 'What about me?'

Again it was David, speaking out at his exclusion, but far more significantly, showing us that he was able to relate to all that was going on. We knew in our hearts that this was a sign, God's sign, that 'this sickness will not end in death, it is for God's glory . . . to give you a future and a hope.' The promises were beginning to come true, and our hearts were rejoicing.

Ann gave David his Communion, and the service ended. It was real and deep and meaningful to each one of us, so much so that we didn't want to leave, but stay and fellowship with each other. But we were in a public ward, and it was now 8.40pm and the nurses wanted us out of the way. The wide curtains had been drawn around the bed for the service but now they were drawn back, and we had to clear the ward. The students returned to Reading, we went back to our home marvelling at what we had heard and seen. It had been a memorable evening.

Now that David had come out of his coma, had emerged from his cocoon, we thought we'd be able to communicate easily. After all, he was now talking, reading, comprehending. He was 'with it'! But was he? He was certainly wide awake in the world of the hospital ward, and knew what was happening all around him. The trouble was that this world was totally unreal, possibly a fantasy, even a dream. There was more hard work ahead.

The first thing that happened was that he wouldn't eat. He refused the food the nurses brought him, and would neither feed himself nor allow himself to be fed. This was distressing, both to the staff and to us. It was irrational and harmful, for he needed the food to build up his physical strength.

Towards the end of the week Donald Lugg came to visit him about tea-time. The evening meal was served but David refused his, pushing the tray away, despite pleadings. Donald soon summed up the situation and decided to do something.

'Well, David,' he said, 'what would you like? Some fish and chips?'

David beamed: 'Yes, that would be nice.'

'Right,' said Donald, getting up, 'I'll be back.'

Off he went to a nearby chip shop, returning soon with two packets of fish and chips wrapped in newspaper. He unwrapped them and offered one to David, who simply wolfed his down in no time; he was really very hungry.

Ann learnt of this when she came in later that evening. She realized then that David was refusing the hospital food but would accept food brought in from outside. She had a word with the sister and arranged to cook a meal at home for David, then bring it in at lunch-time and eat it with him.

It worked. Gently she asked him why he would not eat the hospital food.

'It's poisoned,' he replied, firmly convinced in his own mind.

Again we realized the struggle in his mind to fit the activities of a hospital ward into the reality of life as he knew it. At least he was eating now; but it lay a heavy burden upon Ann who, day in and day out, had to prepare and cook a midday meal, keep it hot, transfer it by car to the hospital, and then sit with him while he ate it. But it meant he had food each day.

The holiday period was over. Maggie was back at her grammar school and our term was about to begin with a new headmaster. With David no longer hovering between life and death, and just about to enter a long recuperative process, it was a little easier for me to tear my mind away from him and to concentrate once more on school work and duties.

My colleagues were co-operative, the headmaster helpful, and my responsibilities were relieved to some extent so that I'd be free to spend an hour with David each day. But it was still a gruelling time. Small boys don't understand about these things — why should they? — and still try to bait their teachers. I found myself becoming impatient, tetchy, unusually annoyed, and then in remorse hating myself for it. The quality of my teaching was affected. Mentally and emotionally exhausted, I found it almost too much to be innovative and creative in my lessons, and I relied more and more on text-book exercises. Yet I taught at a fee-paying school and parents rightly expected more than routine teaching. Noticing this, I resolved to plan at least one innovative lesson per class per week, and this target raised the level of my teaching acceptably.

David, of course, would not be going back to college, and I realized that I had a responsibility to inform the authorities about this. So I wrote to the registrar of Reading University informing him of David's accident, stating that he would not be returning to college this academic year, but expressing the hope that he would be able to take up his place again when he was fit enough to do so; and asking them to waive fees until then. The reply was prompt and positive, expressing concern and compassion, stating that there'd be no fees to pay and that his place at college was assured as soon as he was able to take it up. A few days later came letters of sympathy from his professor and his tutor. Similarly with Kent Education Committee, who paid his fees. Again a letter by return expressing caring concern, and an assurance that his grant would be 'on ice' until he was able to return to college. It was encouraging to find such a human response from an often faceless bureaucracy.

Meanwhile, in some ways David was getting better, in some ways worse. The improvement was physical: although still paralysed down his right side, the rest of his body was now moving. Each day the stalwart physio-therapists put their arms round his waist, and his arms round their shoulders, and 'walked' him up and down, up and down the ward, dragging his paralysed right leg behind him. After ten days of this, the paralysis was beginning to go. He was able to move his arm about, though he dragged his leg still. They took him to the hydrotherapy pool each day and gradually movement returned. Physically he was being restored to wholeness.

But mentally it was a different story and posed all sorts of problems. It was evident that he still hadn't grasped in his mind that he lived in a hospital ward, that he didn't know where he was, or what he was doing there. The first indi-cation came one evening as I said good-night to him at his bedside. He suddenly gave me a punch in the chest. 'Are you real?' he demanded, uncomprehendingly. The con-fusion in his mind must have been quite bewildering. That night he eased himself out of bed, dragged himself across the ward and out of the door, seeking to escape to reality.

But it was too much effort and he was led back to his bed.

The result was humiliating. Cot sides were put on the bed to prevent him getting out and damaging himself. They only served to reinforce his belief that he was imprisoned, as we had to speak to him now through bars. Sometimes he knelt upright on his bed, grabbed the cot sides and rattled them back and forth, bellowing, 'Let me out!' The poor young nurses didn't know how to deal with him, though the experienced sister was well able to cope and to soothe his shattered nerves. We tried every way we could to help him to relate to reality, but how? How?

It was some young friends locally who first made a breakthrough. Two brothers and their sister from a Christian family had been regular in visiting, one or other spending time with David, talking, praying, encouraging him, three or more times each week. It was mid-January now, and there'd been a fresh fall of snow. Sarah, the young girl, visited David one afternoon and talked about this, but he was quite mystified. So she jumped up, asked for a cup, went outside, grabbed a cupful of snow and brought it in to show David.

'Look, David — snow!'

He reached out his hand and felt it. 'Snow,' he said slowly. 'Yes, snow!'

Something penetrated from then onwards; certainly the realization that there was another world outside his own mind.

His speech, though slow and slightly slurred, was improving. At the end of one visit he suddenly said to me: 'Will you pinch me?'

'Pardon?' I said, thinking I hadn't heard aright.

'Will you pinch me?' he said, more emphatically.

I did so, asking, 'Why?'

'I want to know if you're real, if it really is you out there, or if I'm still in a dream.'

Again I tried to assure him that we were solid flesh and blood, and that all was well, all was real.

I wondered how all this would affect his memory; his brain had been damaged — would he suffer from amnesia, and if so, how long would it last?

An opportunity came to put this to the test. There was a television at the far end of the ward, and another test match had begun in Australia. The highlights of the day's play were broadcast at 7.30 in the evening — the last half hour of visiting time. So I helped him out of bed (cot sides down) and assisted him to walk up the ward, positioning ourselves in front of the screen. As players were focused on the screen he named them correctly, stated which county they played for, and recalled accurately some aspect of their playing career. This to me was a most encouraging sign, and of far more interest than the cricket on the screen.

Sarah, who'd helped David to identify snow, and her brother John, were visiting him one day and he was responding to their chatter. Then John noticed that David kept covering one eye with his hand as he spoke to them. He asked Dave why he did it.

'Because I keep seeing two of you,' he answered simply.

When we were told about this we realized he had double vision, which we'd need to do something about as soon as he was fit.

David had been in digs in Reading, and most of his belongings were in the room he occupied in these lodgings. There'd be weekly rent to pay unless we could vacate the room so that it could be let out to someone else. Some of the students in the same digs helped out, putting all his books in cardboard boxes and storing them in their rooms. But there was still the bulk of his personal effects, and a large trunk of clothing to do something about.

Great friends of ours from our own days in Reading were a doctor and his wife whose children were much of an age as ours. They phoned mid-week to say they were free on Saturday and would like to come and see David. Was there anything at all they could do for us? 'Yes, please,' we replied, 'collect whatever you can get into your car from

David's room in Reading, and bring it down here.' This they did, thus freeing us from rent, as well as enabling us to enjoy their company, and for the doctor to assess David professionally.

He spent about forty minutes with him in the ward, without us or anyone else there. As a visitor he did not medically examine him; but he did professionally assess him. His report was encouraging.

'He's not as bad as I thought. He's coming along well, and I don't see why there should not be a 90 per cent recovery at least. He's physically strong and healthy. Mentally he's coming on well. He knows who I am; he converses with me intelligibly; so there's every hope for a full recovery there. It will be slow and painful, but I'm quite pleased and optimistic.'

We were delighted. This was the first prognosis we'd had for a while and it was positive and hopeful.

Meanwhile life went on. Maggie and I tried to concentrate on our respective school-work; Ann cooked a meal for David each lunch time and took it in to him; and Michael cycled to Manston Airport to de-ice the aircraft as conditions dictated. Our faith never deserted us; on the contrary, it upheld us. We knew not only that 'underneath are the everlasting arms' but, in fact (and I mean 'fact'), that they were all around us, hugging us to God Himself in His great caring love for us. We knew now that not only was 'this sickness not unto death', but that the plans 'to give you a future and a hope' were real and true. We knew, too, that the healing had been faster than anyone had anticipated, and we were convinced, not only that our prayers had been heard and answered, but that (even medically speaking) prayer had accelerated the whole healing process. There was much to be thankful for.

But there was a strain, a considerable strain, the brunt of which was borne by Ann. She was back working part-time in the hospital three mornings a week, though not on David's ward. After duty she didn't go straight to see him in her uniform. She went home and changed, freshened her face and appearance, cooked him his lunch, and took it to him on a tray. He would eat it, but then he'd suddenly grab her nose, or pinch her cheeks. 'Are you real?' he would cry out, glaring at her. This happened most days, and added to the burden we carried, but we didn't let it get us down.

Attitude makes a lot of difference. It wasn't that we consciously adopted a hopeful attitude, it was something that sprang up within us. Our positive approach, founded on a living faith, overcame the negative prognosis of others. As Ann walked David up and down the ward, trying to get his paralysed leg moving, a voice called out from a bed, 'You're wasting your time, you know; he'll never get any better. I've seen cases like him before — they never recover.' There are some things that are better left unsaid, and this was certainly one of them. Similarly we had a letter from a friend commiserating with us in David's illness and again assuring us he'd never recover! Both these sources said they knew young people who had had similar accidents, and afterwards they always stole things and behaved quite unpredictably. We determined ·not to be discouraged by such comments, but redoubled our prayers, thanking God for what had been achieved so far, and looking to Him for healing and wholeness.

Attitude does matter, and can affect one's whole approach to suffering. We'd committed David to God's care and keeping, and we rested in that — not fatalistically, though! We worked hard 'to give him a future and a hope', spending hours with him, cooking his food as necessary, indulging his love of cricket, half-walking, half-dragging him up and down the hospital wards: we ourselves had to work at his healing. We did so because we believed in him, we believed and trusted in medical skills, and we believed and trusted in God. Somehow that negative comment from a bed, that unhelpful letter through the post, served to spur us on to more determined effort just to prove them wrong!

Another week passed with gradual improvement all the

time. The physiotherapists, one of whom was a friend whose boys I'd taught, worked hard with him, and the paralysis was less and less pronounced: there was a definite, controlled movement in the limbs now. Ann still brought in food some days, though on others she was able to take him a tray of food from the hospital trolley.

I'd had to arrange an inter-denominational service for the Week of Prayer for Christian Unity in January, and it was set up for the Wednesday evening. We talked about it with David and explained that we wouldn't be in on Wednesday night as we had this service to attend.

'Oh!' said David thoughtfully. Then slowly he asked, 'Can I come, too?'

We were amazed, and didn't know how to answer. The decision was not in our hands. Only Sister could say. When we asked her she wasn't sure either. This was an unusual request. It would mean he'd be out of the ward from 7-9 in the evening; it was all very unorthodox. But the overriding consideration for any patient must be whatever would help them back to health most effectively. So she agreed, provided we kept quiet about it!

Came the Wednesday, we dressed David and helped him walk to the car. We drove to the church and eased him into a chair. He took part, as far as he was able, in that service, insisting on standing for the hymns, and we just marvelled and praised God. It was only two weeks since he'd come out of his coma with the comment 'What about me?' and here he was in a church, worshipping in a service. The promises flooded into my mind: 'This sickness . . . is for God's glory, so that God's Son may be glorified through it.' 'I know the plans I have for you — plans for good and not for evil, to give you a future and a hope!' We knew in our hearts that these promises were being fulfilled in front of our eyes, and we rejoiced. The service over, we delivered a tired David back to the ward, grateful for a further step forward.

III

One Monday towards the end of January, after a ward round, Mr Klugman had a chat with Ann.

'He's really getting on remarkably well. It's quite a miracle.'

Ann smiled to herself, but said nothing.

'He ought to stay in a good bit longer really; but I believe that he might well recover more completely if we sent him home. Now I can only do that provided I am convinced he'll receive a great deal of tender, loving care. That's really the best medicine now. Knowing you as I do, I'm sure he'll receive it. So what do you say? Could you take him home towards the end of this week?'

Ann gasped. This was more than she had dared hope for. 'Yes, fine! I'll have him home as soon as you say!'

'Good. Let's say Thursday afternoon then, after I've seen him in the morning. But I have to warn you of one thing. You mustn't let him out on his own at all. After brain damage like this there's quite a strong possibility of epilepsy, and he might have a fit at any time. So there must always be someone with him — all the time: don't let him out on his own, don't leave him in the house on his own, and never let him come down the stairs on his own. Is that clearly understood?'

'Yes,' Ann replied confidently. 'We'll look after him.'

'I'm sure you will,' said the kindly surgeon, 'and that's why I'm letting him go home early. You see, he's been stripped of his maturity, and it will take time and patience gradually to build this up again; but I'm sure you realize this. He should continue to come here for his physio-therapy three times a week. Can you see about that?'

'Of course,' said Ann, delighted at the prospect of having her son back home.

I had a half day off the following afternoon, and we decided that David would need an upright armchair to sit in, not the deep-cushioned lean-back ones that we had. So we went out to a furniture store, found a suitable one at a reasonable price, and bought it, ensuring that they could deliver it before Thursday afternoon. This was to be David's coming-home present.

Thursday came, and how excited we were! I was stuck at school on my duty day, so Ann collected him that afternoon. After farewells all round and gifts as a token of our appreciation to the dedicated nursing staff, Ann drove David the half-mile home. As he stepped through the front door he beamed like a child and said: 'Now I *know* it's real!'

At long last his two worlds had come together and merged into one, as reality broke through in the familiar surroundings of his own home.

So David came home on 1 February, a month and a half late. He'd been in hospital for seven weeks less a day, and for half that time had been unconscious, almost a third in intensive care. Yet everyone we know in medical circles said it was an amazingly quick healing, far more rapid than usual for such injuries. We knew that the great spiritual force of prayer had been fully brought to bear upon David, and were convinced that this had accelerated the whole healing process.

Coming back from school that evening I reflected on the traumatic event that had, like a stone thrown into a pond, so disrupted the even tenor of family life since my drive home on the last night of last term. I was able to give thanks, heartfelt thanks, for the truly precious things in life: close family ties, supportive friends, skilled medical care, keen church members, committed young people, and understanding colleagues. Together they'd made all the difference in the support we'd received.

It was good to be home. There was David sitting in his new chair, 'clothed and in his right mind' — beside an open fire. He was beaming, grinning all over his bearded face, a look of huge contentment shining from his eyes. No longer the awful 'Where am I?' unknowingness of it all.

David was home, back with his family, back where he belonged, back in reality — and he knew it.

We ate our meal together round the dining-room table, enjoying family chit-chat and banter, watching David tuck in with his usual healthy appetite. The meal over, David got to his feet: 'Now I must do something for you,' he said simply. 'I want to do the washing-up for you!' In the event, of course, we all did it.

The weather was better now, the snow and ice had gone; but it meant that Mike had no job. So he was able to give some time to David, as well as walking the dog and visiting the Employment Centre. Eventually he found a job in a leather factory, a fairly menial task and poorly paid, but it occupied him usefully. He'd just failed to get into the college of his choice, and was waiting to see if another college would have him instead. However, he'd been approved for the post in a Christian guest house in Israel, and would be going there next month, so there was that to prepare — and earn — for.

Contentment reigned: David was home, able to walk, able to communicate, and able to relate to reality. He'd come through his long dark tunnel into the sunlight, and his radiance affected us all. Our spirits and hopes were lifted high, but soon they were to be severely tested.

I wasn't required for games duties that Saturday afternoon and was enjoying the time with the family all together that we'd been deprived of over Christmas. I noticed some people coming up the drive, thought I recognized one of them, but soon decided that it couldn't be. At their knock Mike opened the door and, somewhat embarrassed, ushered in Maureen and her older sister. Maureen fell on David's neck.

'Oh, my darling, how are you? How lovely to see you looking so much better!' she cried.

We were all taken aback. We knew that the strain of this intense relationship was the last thing David should have at this time.

Ann had been preparing tea in the kitchen, but now came in to greet the new arrivals. She took one look at the unexpected Maureen, gasped, and fell to the floor in a faint. More confusion and embarrassment. She soon recovered and her loving hospitality overcame her awkwardness. With a smile she invited the two ladies to stay to tea, which they did. But it was a strained time for us all.

Eventually they left, Maureen asking if she might visit David on Monday, and of course we agreed. But we were worried. The look of tranquillity, of inner peace, that had shone from David's face from the moment he came home was gone, replaced by a tautness, an obvious strain. We wondered how much this would affect his rehabilitation.

David loved worshipping God, and on Sunday we arranged to take him up to the evening service at our church, where John Went was the vicar. It was a service of deep meaning, not least for our family being all together, and of great blessing. John explained afterwards that it was the first time he'd prayed for someone in hospital, only to find him sitting in a pew! David enjoyed the service, and we felt so supported by the church family.

The days came and went. Sometimes we took David out in the car, and then walked around the block with him — a great day. His right leg dragged slightly, but that was all. His strength obviously needed building up, but there was no evidence of an epileptic fit. However, it exercised our minds; here was this active young man, getting stronger and healthier day by day, yet with nothing to do but sit around the house. Ann took him for physiotherapy at the hospital three times a week, which was a useful outlet. However, the doctor had said it would be eighteen months at least before he could go back to college, and we'd only just got past two months.

Yet take him back to college we did — for one night! David had been elected president of Reading University Christian Union as from January, but of course had been unable to take up his post because of the accident. All the previous term the Christian Union had been preparing for a week's Mission to the University, and David had been at the hub of its planning. It took place at the end of February. We arranged to travel down one afternoon, attend the Mission meeting that evening, and come home the next day. As it coincided with my half-term weekend I was able to go too.

It was a remarkable occasion. David received a great welcome from the students, most of whom had last seen him lying in a coma, or caged like an animal. They hugged and encouraged him — and us — and it was a great joy to be part of the Mission meeting, especially for David, who'd helped to plan it. We stayed overnight with a friend and made our way back gently the next day. It was another step forward for David.

Maureen was still coming and going. Gradually our brittle relationship thawed and melted and we were beginning to laugh together; she stayed for a meal with us now and then, and took David out for walks. But it was a strange relationship; David was uneasy and unsure of himself with her, yet fiercely loyal to her. Then she asked David to come and spend a weekend with her, at her home. We weren't too happy about this, perhaps irrationally, but couldn't and wouldn't veto it in a heavy-handed way. So one Friday evening we packed his bags and took him to Maureen's house — she lived with her parents — in Margate. The whole weekend we were on edge without knowing why; David was quiet when we collected him on Monday, didn't say much, and was almost off-hand when we asked him about his weekend away.

Mike was preparing for his journey to Israel, where he'd agreed to work for three or four months at Stella Carmel, a guest house on the top of Mount Carmel above Haifa. He'd failed to win a place at Cambridge, but had secured one at St John's College, Durham. Philosophical and light-hearted as ever, he was looking forward to it positively, especially to joining his great friend Andy Spear there.

David continued to progress and gain strength. But he was restless. As an active fellow, sitting in an armchair day in and day out with nothing to occupy him usefully was not his idea of an ideal life. The embarrassed awkwardness of having to ask someone to go with him whenever he wanted to go out for a walk, or just come downstairs, was, to say the least, quite a bind. So we shared the need for some forms of supervised activity for him with our church family, and two positive offers came.

The first was from a potter who worships with us. He offered David a couple of mornings a week with him in his workshop, an offer eagerly accepted. At school David had excelled at pottery, so much so, that his art master told us that he was the most promising pupil he'd had for a decade. But this same master spoilt it all by putting David in for 'O' level Art, so that, instead of working in clay which he loved, David had had to spend hours swotting up the history of European architecture. He had failed his Art exam, and his love of pottery had been stifled. Here was a chance for it to surface again, as he applied himself to developing once more his creative skills.

The second offer was from a kind couple who had a small plot of land they'd recently bought which had been a commercial garden. It was overgrown now, and the greenhouses were falling apart. Stella, the wife, offered to work alongside David one or two afternoons a week, pricking out plants and getting the place back into shape. She'd even pay him for hours worked.

This was a generous offer which meant a lot to David, helping him to feel both useful and wanted. It was a happy relationship, too, for it had been David's testimony a few years earlier that had brought Stella to a living faith. As a youngster of 17, just out of school, he'd been invited to give his testimony at a friend's house as part of an outreach social evening. Ann and I had gone along and met Stella there. She had seemed nervy and on edge and was rather flamboyantly dressed. She hadn't fitted in with the complacent-looking church meeting regulars, and probably hadn't wanted to. Our host, Bob, had explained a few things, then David had spoken about what knowing Jesus as a friend meant to him, ending simply with the Apostle Paul's words, 'For me to live is Christ.' Stella had been visibly moved and Ann had talked to her afterwards. She admitted to feeling empty inside, and told Ann that David's words had meant a lot to her. The next day she sought out Rosemary Went, the vicar's wife, and expressed her desire to become a Christian. 'If it can all be so real for that young man on the threshold of life,' she'd said, 'it's got to be true!' Rosemary had prayed with her, Stella had asked Christ into her life, and she has been a faithful soldier and servant of His ever since.

So now David had points in the long, lonely weeks, times to look forward to when he could be active and involved. He loved the pottery work, and although the clearing up of the dilapidated greenhouses wasn't exactly exciting, it was a positive activity to engage in.

There was only one dis-ease to disrupt the healthy harmony in the home, and that was the continued relationship with, and regular presence of, Maureen. We were anxious to be charitable, giving her free access to David and our house whenever she wished, and having her frequently to meals with us. But there was still a strain, and David probably felt it most. He withdrew into himself, and we were conscious that at times he was torn between his love and loyalty to his family, and his loyalty and love for Maureen. This was not good for his mental rehabilitation or his emotional well-being. It was a constant topic in our private prayers, as we were aware that it could impede his progress.

March came. David had been home a month, and Mike was due to leave for Israel on Tuesday the 6th. David had been wistfully complaining that he'd missed out on Christmas so Ann, ever the hospitable home-maker, arranged a special Christmas lunch for him, invited Maureen and her own father and stepmother. It was a cheerful occasion. We had turkey and all the trimmings, pulled crackers, wore silly hats, toasted David on his recovery, toasted Mike on his journey, and ate our fill. It was a family occasion to remember, as Ann had meant it to be.

Mike's flight was on Tuesday, so I was free to take him to Heathrow airport. He was glad to have something more permanent and positive to be doing for the next three or four months, and although he was earning only a pittance, he was determined to see and do all he could while in Israel.

Our stresses were by no means over. Maureen went to work overseas, but her mother invited us to come and meet her one evening at home. We were rather wary. It turned out to be an unfriendly interrogation. We were questioned as to why we hadn't looked after David properly since his accident, why we hadn't sent him to a specialist brain hospital in London. We were told that we'd neglected him, deprived him of good medical treatment, and much else in a similar vein. Twice I stood up and made to go, but we were obliged to stay and hear more accusations. It was all very painful, and hurt us both deeply; not so much the half-truths, but the injustice of it all. Fortunately, we were able to recall the remarks of the hospital staff. Nurses, cleaners and porters had said, 'You've been marvellous with your son', 'We've never seen anyone work as hard as you have to get your son better', and so on. Eventually we managed to escape after an hour and a half; our spirits were low and our mouths dry. The prospect of a wedding appalled us. It had been the worst night of our lives. Ann, wounded and hurt, bore the brunt of the pain. We sank into bed exhausted and desolate, too battered and bruised to pray.

The next day Ann awoke shrouded in despondency, her spirits at rock bottom. We usually read *Living Light* Scripture verses each morning, but as I began to read, Ann grabbed the book from my hands and hurled it across the room. '*Where are you, God?*' she cried in her despair.

'You're not here; I don't believe you even exist.' She broke down and sobbed her heart out.

Maggie had made breakfast for us and she and I ate ours, very subdued. Ann would have hers later with David. It was a dull, grey, wet morning, matching our dismal feelings. I went up to see Ann before going off to school. I'd never known her so 'low' before, and I was reluctant to leave her. But duty called; the school had been good in accommodating me during David's illness, and I had a responsibility to go in today. It was my 'duty day' too, and I wouldn't finish until 8pm. I was concerned about leaving Ann for twelve hours. I kissed her goodbye and with a heavy heart went off to work. One consolation, I mused, was that Ann would have to take Dave to physiotherapy today and collect him afterwards. But I sent up arrow prayers for her on my journey and throughout the day. Little was I to know how soon and how wonderfully God was to answer.

I phoned her at break but there was no answer; probably collecting Dave from physio, I thought. I phoned at lunch time and she answered cheerfully. She told me that she'd had a quite amazing visit that morning that had been a great comfort and encouragement to her; she'd tell me all about it when I got home. The day dragged on: teaching, games, more teaching, supervision, prep-duties, marking, lesson preparation. At last duty was done and I sped home on my moped. Ann and I embraced warmly; she said she felt tired now, but would tell me all about her day.

She'd taken David to the hospital for physio, but still felt so low that she hadn't gone shopping as she'd intended. She returned home, knelt down by her bedside to try to pray, but broke into heavy sobbing again. Then the front doorbell rang. She pulled herself together, dabbed her eyes and powdered her cheeks quickly before running downstairs to open the door. There stood a sprightly elderly lady.

'Mrs Hare?' she enquired.

'Yes,' said Ann.

'I don't think you know me, but I know all about you. I'm Mrs Dabbs.'

'Please come in,' said Ann warmly.

The lady folded her umbrella and came inside. Ann was quite sure she'd never seen her before. They sat down together in the sitting-room.

'I belong to the Pentecostal Church,' Mrs Dabbs began, 'and I've heard about your son. I've been praying for him regularly. This morning I was praying for him and the Lord suddenly "spoke" to me, saying, "Go and visit Mrs Hare." "I can't, Lord," I replied. "It's raining!" "You've got an umbrella, haven't you?" the answer came back. "Well, I don't know her, I've never met her before." "Go and see her now." Well, this urge was so insistent I just had to get on my outdoor shoes, find my umbrella and come and see you. The Lord tells me you're in some trouble and need a bit of help.'

It was a lot for Ann to take in. An unknown lady praying for our son for a start. The message from the Lord to visit her, the awareness that she was deeply troubled in her spirit: she must be a messenger from God. She would tell her everything. For the next half hour Ann poured out her heart: David's physical and mental improvement were marvellous and a great source of encouragement and thanksgiving. But his emotional entanglement, Maureen's return and departure, and the ghastly meeting last night — all these, coupled with the tremendous strain of the last three months, had brought her to a very low ebb.

Mrs Dabbs was surely sent by God that morning — praise be for obedient Christians. She told Ann that God knew all about it, that He had David in His special care and keeping, and that He just wanted Ann to trust David into His hands, and He would look after him. She went on to say that she knew she had to give to Ann the words of God to Joshua (8:18): 'The Lord said to Joshua, "Hold out towards Ai the javelin that is in your hand, for into your hand I will deliver the city." ' She showed her an article which pointed out that Joshua's javelin had no military significance or advantage at all; it was held at Ai until it was completely given over to the Lord, in obedience to His Word. We must, she went on, target our prayers for David, completely cover him with God's javelin, claim him wholly for the Lord, until he is completely given over to Him.

Ann knew this must be a word from the Lord, and how He must love her to send someone round at the hour of her greatest need to tell her.

They prayed together. Ann, now consoled and comforted by this complete stranger, yet a member of the family — her sister-in-Christ — was reassured and uplifted. In fact the whole burden of despondency was removed from her shoulders. She embraced her caller warmly.

'I've never done anything like this before,' said Mrs Dabbs. 'Thank you for making it so easy for me!'

'Thank you so much for coming,' said Ann. 'It's meant a lot to me. Now I must go and fetch my son from hospital. Can I give you a lift?'

'No, thank you, I live just over the bridge, and it's stopped raining now.' Sure enough, it had.

It was a remarkable story that Ann told me, and I thanked God for answering my prayers so promptly and so effectively. From that moment on we didn't mention our awful interrogation, and the miserable memory of it was taken from our minds.

April came, and Easter, with its Resurrection promise of new life. It brought warmer weather, school holidays, brighter evenings. Our spirits were brighter, too; we knew we were through the worst with David, and that his continued improvement was just a matter of time. There'd never once been a hint of epilepsy, and the regular physiotherapy was getting his limbs really mobile and active again. There was still a slowness of movement, and a certain lack of co-ordination, but medical staff and lay people kept mentioning his remarkable progress.

David was due to see Mr Klugman for his check-up, so Ann took him along to his consulting room at the hospital. David walked in purposefully, with his slightly lop-sided grin. David Klugman looked him up and down.

'It's amazing,' he said simply.

('Thank you, Lord,' said Ann silently.)

He was very pleased with David's progress, but cautioned us that he wasn't recovered yet. He congratulated Ann on her 'TLC' and said he'd see David again in three months' time. We had much to be thankful for.

But what was poor David going to *do?* How to eliminate the boredom, to give him a purpose, a meaningful activity? Suddenly I had an inspiration.

Down in Devon there is a Christian Holiday Centre called Lee Abbey. Ann and I had been associated with it since its foundation soon after the war, and had stayed there a number of times over the past twenty years. We'd had a family holiday there four years before, when David was 16. It was run by a community of dedicated Christians who offered their particular skills — typing, accountancy, cooking, whatever — to help run the place and share in the life of the centre with the weekly guests. Now Lee Abbey had a farm.

It occurred to me to write to the warden of Lee Abbey (whom we knew) to see if he would take David on the community for three or four months, to work on the farm. He was training in agriculture and had spent some time farming in Kent before reading Agriculture at Reading. It was rather a long shot, but worth a try. I wrote to the warden.

The result was immediate: a phone call came the next day to say that for some weeks they'd been praying for a farm worker to join the community. How soon could we bring David down? (I'd explained in my letter about his accident, and that this would be part of his rehabilitation.)

We arranged a date, the following weekend; we could take him down to Devon and he'd be interviewed as to his suitability to join the community, and his ability to undertake farm work. They would provide accommodation for us all overnight and, provided they felt able to take David on, he could stay, so we would need to bring his belongings.

We were all elated. The prospect of doing something useful, the farming he loved, delighted David. And we were happy for him, seeing this as another sign of God's hand in his healing progress.

In the event it proved to be a delightful and refreshing weekend, a tonic for us, too, in our weariness. The weather was fine and North Devon in late spring was a picture. More important, the warden and farm manager didn't take long to decide they'd be pleased to have David on the community for the next three months: delight all round. It is a mark of Lee Abbey's magnanimity that they were fully aware of the responsibility they were taking on. David still needed to have someone with him all the time.

That evening, after supper, there was country dancing. We were too weary to participate, but Dave wanted to have a go, and with some courage decided to join in. Ann encouraged him, and soon he was enveloped in the swirl and galloping of the dancers.

John Perry, the warden, was at Ann's elbow.

'I've admired the way in which you've gradually withdrawn yourself from David,' he said, 'so that he's no longer dependent on you.'

It was a reassuring comment from a supportive quarter.

The next day we all knelt together at a deeply-felt, reverential Communion service in the beautiful octagonal lounge, with sunshine streaming through the tall window. It was a precious moment of rare deep peace for which we were greatly thankful.

Before lunch there was just time to walk around the gardens, enjoying the sunshine deepening the colours of the steep hills, and sparkling on the water at the foot of the headlands. We met the farm manager, and he showed us around the farm. Then lunch, and our long drive back from coast-to-coast across Southern England; but for the first time in five months, without David.

The three summer months at Lee Abbey were a great tonic for David. He grew in strength, in adaptability, in co-ordination, in companionship. His mental powers seemed unimpaired. We dared to begin to wonder if he could perhaps return to university in the autumn. That would be just nine months since the accident, and Mr Klugman had originally said one and a half to two years before he'd be fit to return to his studies. It really would be a visible miracle if the shortest prognosis was halved!

David was due to see Mr Klugman at the end of June. He'd come home for a long weekend from Lee Abbey to see him on the Friday morning, spend the weekend with us, and return on the Monday. We decided to ask this perceptive surgeon about his prospects for returning to university in September.

Our hopes increased when David came home. His mental and physical readjustment had so obviously improved, his confidence restored. He believed in himself now, and believed that he could cope with the demands and pressures of his university course if he went back in September. One advantage would be that he could 'repeat' the autumn term's work, and so train his mind to pick up again all he'd learnt a year ago, before starting new work in the new year. We prayed that Mr Klugman would agree, realizing that it was a long shot.

In the event, he was so pleased with David's progress that he did agree. He congratulated us on our efforts in David's rehabilitation, though we quietly pointed out that we believed God had a hand in it, too. We thanked him so much for all his care, concern and attentiveness. He told us that although he could not actually forbid David ever to ride a motor cycle again, he would strongly recommend that he did not. David respected his advice and our feelings about this. The bike has been disposed of for ever.

Twelve years later, when Ann had to see Mr Klugman

about her own hip joint, his first words were, 'Hello, how's David?' We owe a lot to a skilled and caring consultant surgeon.

It was time for a celebration! Just six months since he lay motionless, with a cracked skull and in a coma, paralysed down one side, David was pronounced fit enough to return to his studies. This was cause enough for a party. David would be 21 on the first of August, but planned to be overseas with Maureen then. So we decided we'd give him a 21st birthday party the very weekend he was home from Lee Abbey, and he was delighted.

His friends came from Reading, from Thanet, from all around: the young people who'd stood at his hospital bed and tried so hard to get through to him. It was a joyous occasion for them especially, to see him so fit and well. There was music and general rejoicing. Ann, only recently out of hospital herself, had prepared a marvellous spread, with help from kind young friends. David cut his birthday cake — a little prematurely, perhaps — and was enjoying himself immensely, like a schoolboy with his tuck. He was so grateful for everyone's kindness to him, and for their help in his rehabilitation. His university friends gave him a 'deer-stalker' hat, something he'd always wanted. He put it on, beaming with great appreciation at all and sundry as the merry-making continued.

As I watched, my heart overflowed with gratitude to God — not just for my son, of whom I was so proud, not just for His Son, who meant so much to us as a family; especially was I grateful for the way God had carried us through all the trauma and strain of the past six and a half months, with promises from Scripture, with inner assurances, with answered prayer. How impoverished were those who lived their lives without reference to God, I thought, how sad to miss out on faith in Him. How we'd have managed to come through this time without our faith I have no idea.

David went back to Devon, and Mike returned from

Israel. He regaled us with all his exploits, hitch-hiking around that country, travelling down into the Sinai Desert, and even climbing Mount Sinai between 2 and 4am to see the sunrise from the top: an awesome experience. He'd obviously benefited from his stay there. Now he would find casual work before going up to Durham University in the autumn.

David returned from Lee Abbey towards the end of July, and immediately prepared to join Maureen for three weeks. We were somewhat apprehensive about him travelling abroad on his own, but didn't try to stop him. We had misgivings about sending him off to a foreign land, wondering if the positive good of the Lee Abbey sojourn would be undone under the strain of the relationship. But we wanted to be supportive and drove him to the airport.

Three weeks later we collected him and brought him home, where he showed his affection by giving us each a present. Then came September and we drove him down to Reading where he received a great welcome from his friends. Installed in his familiar digs, he soon swung into university life again.

That spring David went up to Scotland lambing, something dear to his heart. He had had a good time overseas, yet he was wondering about his relationship with Maureen. The working holiday in Scotland gave him time to think, away from close friends and family. David was very busy in the day, but he did two weeks' night shift, which meant he was on duty until at least 4am, and back on duty at 10am! In those quiet, still nights with only the sheep for company, he thought deeply.

He came back to Margate for a long weekend before term. On the Monday he was intending to return to Reading, but suddenly decided he would see a local minister if he was free that evening. Well, Andy was free and David talked about his relationship, his rebellion, apparently intensified by our disapproval, and his need to be free. He had borrowed my moped to get to Andy's, but on the way home it wouldn't start, so he had to pedal the three miles home. Once home he was almost in tears. He had friends staying, so he asked us up to our room and told us that his relationship with Maureen was all over. The family cried, with relief, reconciliation and healing.

Maureen accepted David's decision graciously, saying she could not really understand but, knowing the pressure David had been under, it was what she expected. She left him with the message that all she wanted was the best for him. So the long relationship ended by mutual agreement.

David was awarded a 2nd Class Honours degree and we were, perhaps, the proudest of all the proud parents at the graduation ceremony. In his last year at college he'd met an engaging Christian girl, Carolyn, and twenty months later they were married. He and Carolyn now live with their three smashing sons in Reading, where he has a responsible post as a Home Manager in a small charity for people with challenging behaviour. David is an accredited Marriage Guidance Counsellor and Trainer, as well as a District Councillor specializing in issues concerning disability and the environment.

The promises of God, reaffirmed to us so often by Scripture in our darkest hour, had proved true: His plans for David were for good, and had given him a future and a hope. In that confident faith we live; in the God who promises it, we trust. He is our life — and David's!

SECTION TWO

ANN'S STORY

Coming to terms with Cancer

DOUGLAS'S STORY

Coming to terms with Redundancy

ANN'S STORY
Coming to terms with Cancer

It was the Easter holidays. David was still convalescing at home with all that that entailed: keeping him occupied but also keeping a constant though unobtrusive eye on him. The maturity which had been stripped from him at the time of his accident was slowly returning, requiring time, love, and patience in full measure. Maggie was enjoying the respite of the school holidays, for she too had been 'through the mill', and was quite weary. Mike was in Israel, and we rejoiced whenever we received letters from him.

It had been another exhausting day and I collapsed into bed, grateful for its comforting embrace and for the chance to rest; but, as so often happens when one is overtired, sleep did not come easily. I rolled over onto my tummy, hoping that this might induce sleep. As I did so, my hand still on the mattress, I felt a lump in my breast. I fingered it carefully: it was definitely a lump. 'Oh, no!' I thought, 'Not this! I can't face this! I've neither the time nor the energy to cope with this.' I murmured my discovery to Douglas beside me — anxious that he should know, yet not be alarmed by it. 'If you're worried about it, you'd better go to the doctor,' he replied, in a matter-of-fact way. I agreed to telephone the surgery next day, and amazingly drifted off into a most peaceful sleep.

When I woke next morning I was surprised at the peace which I felt. My mother had died of cancer at the age of 48, and I had cared for her and nursed her through her illness. She had suffered a great deal, and it was very distressing for us both. My mother was my best friend. We shared much together, and enjoyed each other's company (I was an only child). Her death had left me with a deep fear of cancer.

I telephoned the surgery. 'I'm sorry, we can't give you an appointment for three days,' was the receptionist's cool reply. Strangely, I was not ruffled, and took the appointment given. When I saw my doctor he moved quickly to arrange a consultation for me with a surgeon, who turned out to be a man whom we both knew.

Michael Butler is a man of few words, yet with a very competent and reassuring manner. Now he showed much compassion and true concern. 'Three out of four lumps are nothing,' he said, 'but we must do a biopsy. Can you come in for it in a week's time?' I explained that we would be taking David to Lee Abbey that weekend, so we arranged for it to be done the Friday after we got back.

I left reassured, but I was realistic enough to know that it still could be cancer. I was grateful to God that He had certainly given me a peace I would not naturally have expected.

There was much to occupy my mind, though. My main concern was to prepare David for a probable stay at the Lee Abbey Community. For now, we realized, it was even more important that he be accepted there.

Our weekend at Lee Abbey was a tonic for both of us, and we rejoiced when the warden called us into his office for a chat, and said that he felt it right for David to join the community for a few months. On the way back from Devon we called in on our doctor friends at Reading. I was able to share with them that I was having a biopsy at the end of the week. 'I always treat a lump with suspicion,' said the doctor earnestly. Fortunately Douglas didn't hear, and I felt it best that he hadn't.

So the biopsy was carried out. The consultant saw me the next morning and informed me that he'd removed the whole lump, and he felt encouraged that it was probably innocent. 'I'd like you to come back and see me next Friday, please,' he said. I went home feeling light-hearted but a little weary from the anaesthetic, and looked forward to a restful weekend.

Tuesday was a glorious May day, sunny and warm with the garden bursting into bloom. I was alone in the house for the first time in almost six months. I felt I had space and could indulge myself with a sit down in the garden enjoying a cup of coffee. I slipped off my shoes and put my feet up — this was luxury indeed. I relaxed as the gentle therapy of the warm sunshine wrapped itself around me. But my tranquil peace was shattered as the telephone rang. 'Bother!' I thought, as I ran barefoot to answer it. The quarry tiles of our kitchen floor struck icy cold on my feet as a voice said: 'Ann, this is Michael Butler here.' I knew at once this meant bad news. 'Could you come up to the hospital this morning, please, instead of Friday?' he went on, trying to sound matter-of-fact.

At that moment it felt as if someone had poured ice-cold water over me. The dreadful sensation went right through me from the top of my head to the bottom of my feet, and down into the stone tiles I stood on. Avoiding the dreaded word that haunted me, I replied, 'That means it's something nasty.' 'Well,' he answered cautiously, 'I'd like to see you now.'

My mind was racing. I thought first of Douglas and then of the family. They'd all had enough to cope with over the past five months. How on earth could I tell them about this? Yet I knew I couldn't protect them from it. Better by far to share the whole thing than try to concoct some kind of hiding game; besides which, I needed their support and prayers.

'How soon do you want me, Michael?' I asked, trying to keep my voice light. 'How long will you be in Outpatients?'

'Till about noon,' he replied.

'I'll try to contact Douglas at school,' I said. 'I'd like him to come with me.' My nurses' training told me that there would be decisions to be made, and we needed to make them in partnership.

I put the phone down. My first concern was to contact Douglas without alarming him too much, and a message via the school secretary would be too worrying. What should I do? I looked at my watch, and realized that it was break-time at school, so Douglas should be in the staff common room. Quickly I phoned the wife of the school chaplain, whom I knew well; she too was a trained nurse, and was sensible, sensitive, and understanding.

I asked her if she'd go to the staff common room and tell Douglas I was needed at the hospital by noon; would he be able to come home, so that we could go together. She found him and gave him the message. Bemused, he couldn't make it out. But it was his half day, and as he had no more teaching commitment he hopped on his moped and came home.

We drove to the hospital immediately. I tried gently to fill Douglas in on what had happened that morning. Michael Butler saw us at once. He smiled softly and kindly, then asked us to sit down.

'I would like to know the truth, please, Michael,' I said firmly, trying to make it easier for him.

'Your biopsy results have come through, and I'm afraid that there is a small cancer,' he said in his gentle yet straightforward way. 'You realize this will mean further surgery; but you have a choice. Either we can do a radical mastectomy or we can remove a section. The decision is yours. I'll leave you for a few minutes while you talk about it.'

I had already realized that there would be decisions to make, but Douglas was bewildered. 'Surely the medical profession makes this kind of decision in the best interests of the patient,' he mused. But I had trained in the days when only radical mastectomies were performed, so it seemed to me this was the way for me. 'If I only have a section removed, I'll always have in the back of my mind that the whole cancer may not have been taken away, and although I will be given very regular check-ups, I'd still have that worry hanging around.'

'Let's ask the consultant what he advises,' said Douglas, still lost.

'All right,' I said, but inwardly I'd made my decision.

The consultant returned. 'Well, what have you decided?' he asked gently.

'Michael,' I said, eyeing him frankly, 'if I were your wife, what would you advise?' Poor man, I'd put him on the spot, and in retrospect maybe it wasn't a fair question. He paused, and a wry smile came over his craggy face. 'Every person is different; I think in our case I'd do a section, with rigid follow-up.'

Strangely, at that moment I knew my own mind was quite made up: for me it needed to be a total mastectomy. I told him so, and he looked at me honestly and approvingly.

'Come in next Friday morning,' he said, 'and I'll operate in the afternoon; you'll be first on the list. Oh, and don't have any breakfast that day.'

The decision had been taken and I was never in two minds about it. Douglas was still bemused; he was weary and angry and in turmoil. Above all, he felt he had a big bone to pick with God. Hadn't we gone through enough as a family already? I felt apprehensive, remembering what a huge operation it had been some twenty-plus years ago when I had been on the wards. But I was grateful to have a surgeon I knew and trusted, and grateful, too, for the many friends who would yet again cover us with their prayers and their love.

As we chatted together, I tried to make light of things. 'We must be thankful for the medical facilities we have, and for dedicated surgeons,' I said. 'After all,' I joked, 'I haven't much to lose — you'll hardly notice!'

Then came the time to tell the family. Maggie would be returning from school that afternoon, and I was determined she should know the whole truth. There was no point in being vague or evasive, for she'd only wonder what was up and probably imagine that things were worse than they really were. Nearly 17, she'd had a lot to cope with these last months. So when she came in from school I told her gently over a cup of tea. But in my anxiety not to beat about the bush I was probably too blunt, too matter-of-fact, and did not give her the opportunity to express her feelings.

Then David and Michael had to be told. We decided that Michael, still in Israel, did not need to be told until after the operation was over, when we'd write about it in an air-letter. As for David, we asked the warden of Lee Abbey to tell him when he felt it right to do so.

My father also needed to be told. I knew he would be upset, for it would bring back painful memories of the past, so I couldn't tell him by phone or letter. I arranged to go to lunch with him and my stepmother in order to tell him personally and gently, face-to-face. I'm sure much hurt is caused by misguided kindness; 'don't let my nearest know, they won't be able to cope' often leads to dreadful tensions, and for everyone involved the terrible strain of pretending and living a lie. Quality living only comes with honesty, love, and a sharing in everything openly.

But there is also a time for everything. On Thursday evening Michael phoned from Israel. It was his 19th birthday, and lovely for us to hear his cheery voice. Yet all my thoughts on openness and honesty went out of the window. We'd decided he didn't need to know until after the operation was over.

Friday morning arrived and Douglas took me to the hospital on his way to school. I felt apprehensive at what I now had to face. I was shown to my bed in a small room with only three beds in it. As I think back, I'm ashamed to say that my first concern was that the mattress was so hard, and this really worried me!

After the routine admission procedure I sat beside the bed trying to read a book. I read the first paragraph over and over again, but I just couldn't concentrate. Then I looked up, and there was a tall man with dark, receding hair beaming at me, his face full of serenity and love. It was John Went, our vicar. How delighted I was to see him. His timing was just right. He sat down beside me and chatted and prayed with me for a whole hour, simply sharing

God's healing love and peace with me in a way I shall never forget. He told me that his wife Rosemary had invited several ladies from the church to come to the vicarage to pray for me at the time of the operation, as well as for the surgeon and medical team. I was overcome by such love and care, and was encouraged that all would be well.

At two o'clock I was wheeled down to the operating theatre, very aware that the peace I had could only come from God Himself.

I awoke feeling very sick, with tubes coming out of my side and a drip into my hand. I asked a passing nurse what time it was, and was amazed to find it was Saturday morning.

In no time I was being hoisted out of bed and made to sit in my bedside chair, whereas all I wanted was to rest and relax and wallow in my bed, to relieve the pain and bear the sickness. Then I was given an injection and, quite suddenly, just before lunchtime, I felt much better. I managed to eat a little lunch, and then was helped back into bed. I felt fine now, and so, when Douglas arrived, I sent him to fetch Maggie (I had told her not to come while I was feeling rotten). By then I was feeling quite perky, and it was good to have their companionship. They found it hard to believe that I should be so well, so quickly.

It was interesting to be on 'the other side of the bed', to hear and watch, to long to give a hand, sometimes to ache at things said and done, at other times to rejoice at such tenderness and patience. My nurses' training and instinct made it difficult at times for me not to comment on some insensitive attitudes. We were all sent to sit in the day-room each day, where we had to endure the constant television. Occasionally I crept back to my bedside chair to have a quiet read, but usually I was sent back to the day-room like a naughty child.

Although I felt reasonably well, I did have considerable pain from the drain site in my side, and needed pain-killers every four hours. On Sunday the nurse brought the drugs round at 6pm but the pain-killers had run out. 'I'll send to another ward for some,' she said. An hour later a friend arrived to see me. I tried to chat and laugh, but the pain was getting worse and worse. 'You're in some pain, Ann,' she realized. I explained that the tablets should be coming, but I had been waiting for well over an hour. She very kindly went to investigate. 'Just coming!' she was told. Hoping that this was so, and sensing my discomfort, she slipped away. Another hour passed, and the pain was hardly bearable. I rang my bell . . . a hasty apology and ten minutes later I had my drugs to my great relief — but it was then long after 9pm.

A couple of days later the staff nurse came to me and said: 'You really shouldn't be having all these pain-killers,' — as if I was taking them just for pleasure. I told her the pain was intense, but she retorted, 'You shouldn't be having pain now.' How I wished that that was so! I thought I knew the reason; the drain was pressing on a nerve. 'Once the drain is removed, then the pain will go,' I said. I don't think she believed me, but two days later when the drain was taken out so, with it, went all trace of pain.

On Thursday afternoon I had unexpected visitors. A dear friend with whom I'd trained as a nurse travelled with her husband from South London to see me. We'd been through a number of ups and downs together, and were very close. She was, in fact, David's godmother. We were talking animatedly together as she unpacked some goodies she'd brought for me, when a solemn young man arrived at the foot of my bed; 'I'm from the appliance department,' he announced flatly, rather like the man from Kleeneezee.

My friends took themselves off briefly while the Kleeneezee man started talking about prostheses, and in a matter-of-fact way showed me his wares. Somehow the ludicrous situation of this earnest salesman offering me different sizes and shapes of artificial breasts got to me. 'Oh,' I said, 'you really disappoint me; I thought at least you'd show me one

I could blow up!' But he didn't blink an eyelid, and left after making an appointment to see me in Out-patients.

My friends returned and together we enjoyed a good laugh about it. If you can laugh about a problem you can begin to deal with it. I was fortunate to know myself secure and accepted in God's love, to be surrounded by a supportive family, an understanding and loving husband, and to have good friends to laugh with. But I was concerned for those not so secure and fortunate as I was. Surely the appliance person for mastectomy patients needed to be a sensitive and caring lady — a recommendation I later made to the hospital.

A week and one day after the operation I was ready for discharge. It was a Saturday. Douglas would be able to come and collect me after morning school, and slowly I would get back into 'working order'. My kind friend from South London wanted me and Maggie (whose half-term it was) to come and stay with her for the week, and local friends said that they would bring me home afterwards. They would look after me in their house for a few days more before I finally 'got stuck in' at home.

The Friday evening before I left, the ward sister looked in to say 'Goodbye' as she was off for the weekend.

'When will I get the results of my gland biopsy?' I inquired.

'In about another week,' she replied, 'but I don't think you need worry.' Then she added airily, 'Mind you, I wouldn't be in your shoes for anything!'

Had I heard aright? I was quite stunned. This is hardly the sort of remark one expects to hear from a professional nurse to a patient.

Two weeks later I had an appointment with the consultant to hear the results of the biopsy, though as I'd had no phone call I felt all was well. I was right — and what a relief it was! I was one of the fortunate ones — no need for further treatment. Regular follow-up, yes, but nothing more.

75

About this time, after-care for mastectomy patients was much in the news, and there was a documentary programme about it on television too. I watched with indignation as a 'poor me' attitude was portrayed. 'Goodness me!' I exclaimed, 'I'd have more to complain about if I'd lost a leg or an arm! We're the lucky ones; we can have a breast removed and no one need know. It isn't debilitating in any way!' I felt a positive approach would be much more helpful, and I've always been grateful that my cancer was caught early.

The Mastectomy Society was very helpful, and eventually fitted me with an appropriate prosthesis — a size minus 1A, I think!

At first, whenever I met someone for the first time since my mastectomy, I always noticed their eyes swivel towards my chest. I would smile to myself and wanted to say aloud, 'No, it doesn't really show, does it?'

That was fourteen years ago, and since then I've visited many pre- and post-operative mastectomy patients. I always try to go looking 'my best', to encourage them that one can live a very full and normal life after a mastectomy.

DOUGLAS'S STORY
Coming to terms with Redundancy

It was the middle of the winter term, 1981. Ann was fully fit, busy running the home and active in church life. David was in his final year at Reading University; he had settled down remarkably well to his studies, and was busy writing the dissertation to be submitted for his final examinations in the summer. Michael was in his second year at St John's College, University of Durham, and loving every minute of it. Maggie had not managed to get the grades she needed in her final exams to be admitted to teacher training college, but had been accepted into the sixth form of the senior school at the college where I taught in the junior school. With God's help we had picked ourselves up, individually and as a family, from the double blow of David's devastating accident, and Ann's sudden mastectomy, and life was continuing on a more even keel. Yet I was uneasy, apprehensive, and becoming more and more unsettled at school.

The headmaster who had started two years before, when David was in hospital, soon realized that he'd taken on a very complex and difficult job. Within a year he'd tendered his resignation. For two terms the second master from the senior school was acting head of the junior school while a new headmaster was being sought. Eventually a new man was appointed to start in September 1980. But much damage had been done. Within four years we'd had three different headmasters, plus two acting heads. Such a situation does not engender stability, even credibility. Not unnaturally the goodwill of the parents was rapidly evaporating, and the number of pupils was falling considerably. The senior staff were stretched to the limit to keep things going and were quite exhausted; morale, though not utterly low, was not exactly high. The new head would have, as a first priority, to restore confidence among a jaded staff and disillusioned parents.

A private school is as much an economic unit as an educational institution. There must be enough pupils attending for it to be viable as a school at all. The new headmaster certainly worked hard to win friends and influence people. But the numbers remained depressingly low. There was a well-founded rumour in the staff common room that two members would probably be made redundant, given the decreasing number of pupils. The two more recent recruits were those most likely to go; and I felt sorry for them both.

One Saturday towards the end of term, I'd finished my

duties by early evening and set off for home on my moped. I was preaching in chapel the next day, so needed to get home to complete my sermon preparation.

It had been a tiring week, and I needed to revive my flagging energies. I was half-way through tea when the phone rang. I answered, and was surprised to hear the headmaster on the other end of the line. 'Douglas? I've been trying to find you. I've something to say to you.'

'Yes?'

There was an awkward pause. Then, 'I want you to come back to school, so that I can tell you personally.'

'Come back to school — now?'

'Yes, please. I want to see you at once.'

I put the receiver down, quite mystified. After telling Ann I'd been summoned back, I set off for the fifteen-minute ride to school.

'Come in, Douglas,' said the head, rather stiffly, as I arrived.

He seated me in front of his big desk and went and sat himself behind it. He seemed somewhat awkward and ill-at-ease, and I felt like a naughty schoolboy as I faced him across the desk. 'What on earth is all this about?' I wondered.

He looked at me rather nervously and said, 'I've written out what I want to say to you so that I get it right, and I'm going to read it to you now.'

He held up a piece of paper and read: 'At their meeting this morning the Governors have reluctantly decided that because of the falling numbers of pupils, the contracts with Mr Richard Johnson and Mr Douglas Hare will have to be terminated as from the end of the summer term — that is, on 31 August 1981.' He read on, about adequate compensation and the like, but I wasn't listening any longer. The cold douche of his pronouncement had numbed me. 'You're being made redundant, Hare; you're being given the boot!' I had to keep telling myself, yet I still couldn't believe it.

The head put his piece of paper down, and began to speak without his script.

'I'm sorry to have to tell you this. I've told Richard Johnson already, of course. I wanted to leave it to the end of the day, but then I couldn't find you. Of course, we'll do all we can to help you find other employment. You'll be fully compensated. See the bursar about that next week, will you? I don't know if there's anything you want to say . . . .'

I was too stunned to react, still trying to take in what I'd heard. Anyway, what *do* you say? I mumbled something, I know not what, and walked out.

Driving home on my moped, my helmeted head was in a whirl. So the dreaded redundancy axe had fallen on Dick Johnson and me — both senior housemasters, both subject heads as well. More grimly for us, each of us was approaching our mid-50s, with the prospect of getting another job greatly reduced. It was very hard to believe.

It was for Ann and Maggie, too, though Ann, with her feminine intuition, had guessed that something was up. I tried to look on the positive side: five months to try to get another job; released from a school where I'd been increasingly uneasy. But there wasn't much joy in either of those, for they were soon quelled by the daunting prospect of searching for and finding a job at my late age, and the sad realization that I'd be cut off from my colleagues, pupils, and their parents, most of whom were friends, at a school where I'd worked and served and which had become part of my life for thirteen years.

My mind and emotions were in a turmoil, and I felt misplaced anger towards the new headmaster. It is never easy to pass on bad news; there's no 'right' way to tell someone that he or she is redundant. The instant reaction is to blame the messenger for the message, and I fell easily into this trap. Anger and the beginnings of bitterness began to develop, and some very unChristian thoughts and feelings. Yet despite another hammer-blow, life must go on.

I managed to concentrate for an hour on polishing up my sermon for the next day's chapel service — fortunately most of the preparation had been done during the week. We'd been invited to a party, and after some indecision decided to go: it might help to take us out of ourselves, instead of brooding on what had just happened, and the way it had been done. Of that party I remember not a thing. I must have been a very damp squib indeed, though Ann, as always the sparkling catherine-wheel, more than made up for me. What I do remember is the next day preaching in the school chapel one of the best sermons I've ever given. I really felt gripped by the Spirit of the Lord, and empowered from on high. I needed to be; in myself I was still stunned and reeling from this knock-down blow. Yet God had shown me, if I had eyes to see, that He was still in control. If He could equip me for the demands of the present, He could equally well be trusted for the uncertainties of the future.

So again, for the third time in three years, we were facing loss. In David's case it was — miraculously — only temporary loss of faculties, consciousness and time. In Ann's instance, loss of part of her body. Now we faced the loss of job, of income, of dignity. But, as with David and Ann, there was more to it than that. I enjoyed teaching, and had been doing so for thirty years; the class-room was, so to speak, my natural habitat. I liked the task of communicating fresh ideas, of teaching new skills, of training different techniques. I appreciated the uncomplicated enthusiasm of pre-adolescent boys, and the challenge of channelling all that eager energy into worthwhile pursuits, in and out of the class-room, on and off the games field. Teaching is not just telling. It's communicating knowledge obviously; but the communicator is a person, not just a textbook nor a computer screen, nor an audio tape. At its best, teaching is a personal sharing of knowledge or skills, and so a relationship develops; and if there is that personal element, the teacher is *ipso facto* sharing something of himself: his standards, his values, his beliefs. And that's the excitement and challenge of teaching. All this I was to lose.

That Sunday afternoon I reflected about my own teaching career, which now seemed blighted. As a young man I was shy, introverted, and greatly lacked self-confidence. But a conversion experience at college gave me a confidence in God that has never deserted me. This, in turn, enabled me to believe that God had a confidence in me (of all people), and so if He believed in me, then I could believe in myself. When I offered my life to God for His service, I knew with an inner certainty that He desired me to be a schoolmaster. So I came to teaching as a definite calling — literally — and this undergirded all my training and practice. Obviously it took time to develop, and when I began my teacher training course at the London University Institute of Education, I was still nervous and hesitant, and it was touch-and-go whether I'd be able to handle a class.

I'd grown greatly in confidence and ability since my training days, and I loved my profession. I hadn't gone into teaching as one of a number of options, nor because I didn't feel capable of doing anything else (as Bernard Shaw's cruel aphorism, 'Those who can, do; those who can't, teach' implies). I'd become a teacher as a definite vocation; I believed that this was God's calling for me, that this was what He'd equipped me to do and to be. So what was He asking me to do now, after thirty years as a professional teacher? What did the future hold. Or, rather, and more importantly, what was His plan for my life? For my part, I had no idea.

Richard Johnson and I shared the same study, and so talked endlessly. We'd both served in Nigeria in colonial days — Richard as aide-de-camp to the governor, me as a teacher training tutor and vice-principal. We'd both been appointed to the school at the same time, so we both had thirteen years service there; but because of our service abroad, neither of us had a full pension. We went to see the bursar together, a friendly chap, and were told that the school would give us the exact compensation as required by law.

Richard decided to challenge this, and wrote to the chairman of the Governors. He pointed out that a boarding-school master gives himself to the life of the community, always going the extra mile: after-hours activities, preaching in chapel, taking boys on the Broads in school holidays, and much else. He said that the school should recognize this and should, therefore, be more fulsome with its gratuity. To their credit the Governors accepted his case, and more adequate compensation was granted to us.

Somehow I stumbled through the rest of the term. I tried hard to throw myself into my work, and partly succeeded. After all, boarding-school life does not allow many minutes in the day to withdraw and contemplate. However, the motivation for dedicated service had been gravely undermined, and the easy temptation to be slack was ever present. What kept me going was not burying myself in books or paperwork. It was people. The sympathy and understanding of colleagues, together with the innocence and enthusiasm of the boys — these were what mattered.

As a housemaster I had fifty or so boys whose character and classroom development it was my responsibility to monitor. That meant cultivating a fairly friendly and relaxed relationship. Of course, 'boys will be boys', but a boarding school is a 'home from home' for the pupils, and so a homely atmosphere of care, concern, and interest is essential in order to sustain a happy environment. One of the best headmasters I knew was, in fact, still a schoolboy at heart; he revelled in laughingly thumbing his nose, making awful puns, and sending round witty cartoons to his staff. He never minded harmless naughtiness, and even had a photograph on his study wall of two boys thoroughly enjoying a pillow-fight in the dormitory — an event he was as likely as not to have joined in himself! But swearing, bullying, stealing, cheating and lying he would not tolerate

— and the boys knew it. They loved him, and his school was one of the happiest I knew.

I tried to make the most of the last term, and to enjoy the winsomeness of boisterous boys, the cricket games and matches, sports day, and even the class-room routine. Yet there were days when I felt really depressed, when the sense of loss was almost overwhelming. At such times school seemed a menace, and I droned wearily through the long hot day, out of sorts with myself, with colleagues, and with pupils. My fellow teachers were most understanding and supportive, always willing to stand in for me if I went off in search of a job. One colleague, also a housemaster, was so appalled by our redundancy that he decided to quit, and handed in his notice, even though *he* would not be getting any redundancy payment!

Every week I wrote here, there, and everywhere for other posts: schoolteaching, Christian education, church administration — but with a nil response from them all. Term eventually ended. Richard and I were given a hearty farewell. I was particularly delighted when the boys in my house gave me a silver tankard, suitably engraved. As there was no need for me to be involved in the planning meeting for next term I went home, sat down, and took stock. I had eight weeks holiday with pay, plus my 'lump sum' redundancy payment, but no prospect of any job in sight.

I went to see my building society manager about the mortgage, my bank manager about the imminent end of a regular income, and the job centre manager about prospects for employment. Each was sympathetic and, in his own way, as helpful as he could be, without solving any problems. Then I went to see my vicar.

John Went was a marvellous man. A true pastor of his flock, an inspiring preacher, and a tireless worker, he had built up his church through love and care, through effort and vision and yet more love. It was a church that was growing, outward-looking, seeking to serve others. A church should not be 'a place to which people go', but a community to which they belong. The distinction is vital: the former is passive and lifeless, the latter active and caring, outgoing and mutually supporting; and by its very nature it attracts others — and the 'others' were beginning to be attracted.

John had been a tower of strength to us, too — during Ann's operation, during David's long illness and his emotional entanglement. Not only supporting us personally, but mobilizing his church to pray for us, as well as arranging the very practical help of meals with others and at his own home. So I went to a close friend who was also my warm minister, a brother in the Lord, as well as a pastor of his flock.

After the pleasantries I blurted out: 'John, I've been made redundant!' His jaw dropped. 'You haven't! Not from — '

'It's true,' I said.

'Well, isn't that amazing! It's almost unbelievable.'

'I've found it hard to believe; yet in an odd way, I feel a sense of release about it.'

We chatted on, but I could tell that John's mind was racing ahead. He asked if I'd got any prospects, or any job in sight.

'None at all,' I replied gloomily, 'and that's not without trying. No one's interested in you once you're over 50!'

He smiled, and became quite animated. 'We're a growing church here, with a large number of fringe members. I can't get to the fringe at all, and I'm aware they're falling away. So about six months ago the PCC discussed the possibility of appointing a lay worker as a full-time member of staff — the numbers justify it. The PCC decided they'd like to, but there was no suitable candidate. I could see you and Ann filling the role ideally. Would you be interested?' He leaned forward and looked at me owlishly through his spectacles. He was earnest, but there was a soft smile about his lips.

'I'd love to,' I replied; 'nothing would give me more

pleasure than to work full-time for the Church. But I'm afraid I can't, John. I must have an income: I've still got a mortgage, and because of our missionary service overseas we've only half a pension and no savings. So you see, I have to seek paid employment.'

'That's all right,' he replied, to my amazement. 'We'll see about that. I'll have to check with the Church wardens and Standing Committee, and then with the full PCC. We've already talked about employing someone, and if they know you're available I'm sure they'll agree. No, that's all right. We'd pay you a proper salary.'

'How?' I asked.

'From funds, from the congregation. I expect we'd set up a Ministry Fund, and ask people to contribute to it.'

Once again, though in a far happier context, I could not believe what I was hearing. I'd gone to see my vicar for consolation, and here he was offering me a job. Not just any job, but one I could really enjoy and be fulfilled in. I'm a cautious chap and need to talk things over and think them through before rushing in to commit myself, and of course John could not commit himself. He had to test his idea with his Church wardens and PCC, but we were both excited by the prospect.

At lunch-time I talked it over with Ann, who was, as always, reassuring and supportive. One bonus of this job offer, of course, was that it would mean we wouldn't have to move, whereas almost any other job would entail that. We decided to continue to explore other avenues, to apply for any realistic openings, but to be fully open, too, to Holy Trinity's generous offer.

One difficulty was the somewhat anomalous position I'd be in as a full-time paid worker at an Anglican church, who was neither the vicar nor the curate, nor even a minister at all. If this confused me, it certainly confused everyone else; so it would need to be sorted out. I was already a licensed lay reader, which meant that I could take services and preach sermons, but on a voluntary, unpaid basis. Apart from the deaconesses (as they were then called), the Church of England did not know much about *paid* lay workers, certainly not male ones. John Went's imaginative idea to appoint me as a lay assistant minister was great, but would it be accepted in the Diocese of Canterbury, ever cautious and reluctant to be seen to be creating a precedent? Furthermore, John may get the agreement of his Church wardens and Standing Committee, but his full PCC would not meet until mid-September, so I could hardly be appointed before the beginning of October. Yet I'd be out of work, without any income, from the end of August. So while enamoured with the idea, and animated by the prospect, we still felt it right to pursue other channels for employment to see if anything else opened up for us.

At the same time, of course, we prayed. As committed Christians we believed that God not only took an interest in our lives, but as a caring Father who loves His children, He wanted the best for us. We need to recognize that our best may not be His best — in other words, what we consider is best for us (or even second best) may be quite different from God's idea. In the very nature of things He is on a totally different plane of existence from us mere mortals, and sees things totally differently: '"For my thoughts are not your thoughts, neither are your ways my ways" declares the Lord.' (Isaiah 55:8.) Yet God is not remote from us, He doesn't distance Himself from us. The prophet goes on: 'This is what the high and lofty One says, he who lives for ever, whose name is holy: "I live in a high and holy place, *but also* with him who is contrite and lowly in spirit, to revive the spirit of the lowly and to revive the heart of the contrite. . . . I have seen his (wilful) ways, but I will heal him; I will guide him and restore comfort to him."' (Isaiah 57:15, 18, emphasis ours.) We believed assuredly that God would guide us because He lived within us.

The end of August came, and all the letters of application had drawn a complete blank — often not even an acknowledgement, just silence. So on 3 September I went along to the euphemistically-titled Unemployment Benefit Office, and joined the dole queue. It was a very salutary experience. There were many levels of emotion operating in that small office so that the air was supercharged. Frustration, anger, despondency, resignation — all were present, writ large on people's faces. There was a full age-range of people — mostly men, but youngsters the age of our children jostling with skilled workers in middle age, or professional people like me in their 50s or even 60s. Also there, with strained faces, were young executives and elderly labourers. I stood in the queue and watched the sad scene, absorbing the anxious atmosphere. 'It wouldn't hurt,' I thought, 'for ministers — both of the Crown and of the Church — to have to go through this.'

The officials were pleasant enough, but quite obviously, and naturally, distanced themselves from their clients. My first mistake, I was firmly yet politely told, was not to have reported on 1 September — my first day of unemployment. As a result, I would lose two day's benefit. I just accepted this without protest.

This was a different world from mine. I'd never been unemployed before in thirty years of working life. I'd never been paid before on a daily basis nor had a weekly wage. It had always been a monthly salary. I was rightly taken down a peg or two. So now I was registered as unemployed and sent to the Professional Employment Bureau to see if they had any possible jobs to match my skills and training. They hadn't, but would get in touch with me if/when they had. I left with mixed feelings: grateful to a government who makes financial provision for its unemployed work-force, but disgruntled at the system which makes one feel humiliated, reinforcing the inner feelings of rejection and failure. It would seem that something more positive and affirming is needed as well as the basic financial benefit. As in so much in life, it comes down to attitudes.

By mid-September I was another statistic on the unemployment register, and receiving unemployment benefit. Then the Church wardens, Standing Committee and Parochial Church Council of Holy Trinity Church all unanimously agreed to their vicar's suggestion that I be employed by the Church as a full-time lay pastor as from 1 October. Our immediate future was secure. I suggested to John Went that both for his (as well as his Church's) sake and for ours, we said initially that the contract should be for one year, to be reviewed in six months. This gave a 'let out' to each of us if it didn't work out, or if I had the opportunity to return to teaching. I also asked if both Ann and I could be commissioned together at the evening service on Sunday 1 October. John readily agreed, and suggested asking the Archdeacon of Canterbury (whom he knew) to do the commissioning.

So it was that on the last day of September we took Maggie, our youngest, to the teacher training college of her choice to settle in as a first-year student. (She'd got an 'A' grade in her 'A' level exams which she'd failed six months before!) We returned that evening to a childless home for the first time since the birth of our first-born, twenty-three years earlier. The next evening, at a memorable service with over a hundred present, Ann and I were duly commissioned at the Chancel steps by Archdeacon Simpson to serve God in the parish; and the congregation undertook to support us by their prayers, by their presence, and from their pockets. It was a moving occasion, and many felt that it was a step forward in the life of the church.

We were given three main tasks: to visit every home (800 plus) on a new housing estate in the parish; to develop the eight home groups; and to foster contacts with the 'fringe', who came to our church only occasionally. It was a happy and rewarding work. It is a privilege for a Christian to share his faith and to witness to his Lord, to seek out the needy and to show the compassion of Jesus, to preach the Gospel and to proclaim God's love to individuals. Such a ministry bears its own fruit: the joy of response and the sorrow of indifference; the heart-warmth of interest and the heartache of disappointment. The privilege of exercising such a ministry is its own reward. So, just one month after my redundancy, I was being paid to exercise this ministry, together with my life partner, in our own church. Who could doubt that God had brought us through the dark days to fulfilment in His service? The people dipped into their pockets to support us, and the treasurer told me some time later how he was constantly amazed that there was just enough in the Ministry Fund each month to pay my salary. Ann worked voluntarily and was unpaid.

Twelve years on, two vicars, two interregna, and four curates later, Ann and I are still exercising this same ministry together in the same church. The home groups have grown to twenty-four, and we have laid the foundation stone for a new church to be built on the housing estate. The Diocese has taken on the responsibility for my salary, thus easing the burden on the congregation. So we see God's hand upon our lives, and the redundancy — so devastating and unsettling at the time — was turned into a rewarding ministry in His time. We both feel within ourselves that we are in the place God wants us to be, using the gifts He's given us, and doing the job He wants us to do — for Him!

SECTION THREE

MICHAEL'S STORY

Coming to terms with Tragedy

I

The postman came early on Saturday morning, 16th January 1988, and rang the doorbell. By the time I'd jumped out of bed, found slippers and dressing-gown, got myself downstairs and unlocked the door, he'd gone. He'd left a large package on the doorstep, covered in stamps — Canadian stamps. I grabbed it eagerly and took it upstairs for Ann to open. It was a photo album from Mike and Catherine, with photographs of their first child, James Edward Henry Hare, from the moment of birth almost, just two months ago to the day, right through their Christmas with Catherine's family. We enjoyed the luxury of a cup of tea in bed, and we glowed with pride as we looked at the pictures of our latest grandson and his adoring parents.

Mike was now a staff worker for Inter-Varsity Christian Fellowship, based at McMaster University, Hamilton, Ontario, but with responsibility for a smaller university as well. McMaster alone had 15,000 students, and he loved his job, getting alongside the students in their social, cultural and sporting life, and especially in supporting, training and encouraging the Christian students in their outreach and in their personal growth as Christians. It was a demanding and fulfilling job, very much what the individual made of it, but Mike had won his spurs and so impressed his superiors that they had appointed him a regional director, the youngest in their history.

There was a letter from Mike in the package, telling us about their Christmas, and about his schedule for the next six to eight weeks, including a skiing and Bible study weekend up at 'Grandad's Cottage' in Owen Sound, 15-17 January. However, mostly his letter was about his pride and joy in his little boy, which the pictures bore out. 'Altogether', he wrote quaintly, 'he's a great all-round chap to have around the place' — an endearing comment, but unusual for describing a baby just seven to eight weeks old. It was something I was to remember for a long time.

We realized that today he would be with a group of students, skiing together by day and studying the Bible together in the evening, and we prayed for them. It was a heart-warming start to the day and we tackled our jobs with enthusiasm. I retired to my study to work on the morrow's sermon, while Ann busied herself around the house and garden.

In late afternoon we had some tea together and prepared to go up to church for the forty-minute prayer meeting for tomorrow's service. I reckoned there'd be enough time that evening to finish off and revise my sermon, and then to have a good bath.

Though there weren't many at the prayer meeting it was a real and meaningful time together. It was led by Colin, and we prayed deeply and realistically for every aspect of the next day's four services, especially the preaching of the Word. I was glad my sermon had a prayer base for the preaching.

As we opened the front door the phone began to ring; Ann answered. It was David. In a thick voice he said, 'Can I speak to Dad, please?'

'Yes, dear,' said Ann, somewhat surprised. 'Is anything the matter?'

'Can I speak to Dad, please?' he replied, more insistently.

'It's Dave,' said Ann. 'He wants to speak to you.'

I gave a wry, semi-nervous chuckle, as I wondered what my son needed to talk to me about, rather than his much more practical mother. 'Hallo, Dave!' I said cheerily.

'Dad — Michael's dead!' His voice was thick and heavy. This just didn't register: Who's this Michael? It was no one in Carolyn's family. Was it their lodger, an uncle who'd been ill, even a favoured pet? I was bewildered: 'Michael?' I asked querulously, innocently, 'Who? Which?'

'Michael — my brother!' he replied hoarsely, in a shaky voice.

I felt my knees begin to buckle as the awful truth dawned. I was still bewildered how news about our son in Canada had got through to Dave without coming first to us. I felt mentally confused and emotionally pole-axed.

'Our Mike — dead?' I blurted out in my bewilderment, thereby unwittingly letting Ann know.

'Yes,' Dave replied. 'Catherine's been trying to phone you. She couldn't get hold of you and so rang me. There's been a terrible car crash. He was driving a minibus with some students, and it skidded on ice and crashed into a lorry, and Michael's dead.'

I was trying to take this in, and felt sick in the pit of my stomach; my knees were still shaking. I'd had enough and noticed that Ann was naturally agitated.

'You'd better speak to your mother,' I said, and slumped against the wall.

David explained to Ann the circumstances and how Catherine had eventually phoned him. He'd carried the awful information alone for an hour, trying every few minutes to phone us. He'd phoned Colin to discover our whereabouts, and left a message with Sarah his wife; so Colin would know when he got back home from the prayer meeting. Eventually David rang off, relieved to have shared his burdensome news, after we'd said that we'd be in touch again and that we would tell Maggie. Ann put the phone down and we fell into each other's arms. 'Oh, that poor girl, that poor, poor girl,' said Ann, characteristically not thinking of herself, but of Catherine, Mike's young wife, now an early widow, with a baby to look after on her own.

As the grim news and its impact gradually enveloped us, Ann and I moved from the hall into the sitting room. We held on close to each other for mutual support but said little. There were no tears from either of us. We were still too stunned, still in a state of shock, emotionally paralysed. I felt a huge heaviness come over me, and with it a chilling lethargy. Then Ann, practical as ever, began to think ahead. 'We must all go out for the funeral,' she said. 'All of us — Maggie and David as well. We may have to ask for help or to sell some furniture, but we must all go — whatever the cost.'

'Yes,' I readily concurred.

'What about Maggie? How shall we tell her? We really ought to be there with her; she and Mike were so close. I really wonder . . . .' She paused, and looked at me quizzically. 'I wonder if we shouldn't wait till tomorrow, and tell her ourselves. It's a nasty foggy night, I don't think we should try to drive there now. There's no need to go tonight and, besides, we don't know when she will be in this evening.'

I felt chilled and drained and heavy-laden. The one thing I knew for certain was that I couldn't drive to Southampton this dark, wet, January night. I just thought of our son: a fine, upright, good-looking, God-fearing young man. His well-built athletic frame was crowned with an open face, smiling blue eyes and blond hair. He had an easy-going nature which belied a disciplined inner life. He was master of himself, but always open to others — a happy combination of qualities. We were so proud of him — as proud as he was of his own new son. Then his own words about his own boy came back to me; 'Altogether, he's a great all-round chap to have around the place.' Yes, Mike, that was you, too. These words are your own epitaph for yourself!

'What do you think?' Ann broke in upon my reverie.

'What? Yes — no! No, we can't go to Southampton tonight; that's for sure. Neither of us is in a fit state to drive at the moment. Yes, we'll drive down tomorrow, and tell her ourselves. I'll probably be able to get off my sermon — I doubt if I could preach it anyway — yes, I'll have to get off that.'

'Then we could go down tomorrow morning and see her,' Ann continued, 'and bring her back here. We don't know when the funeral will be, but it will probably be next week; we may have to fly on Monday or Tuesday; we don't know. So if we go down to Southampton in the morning, we can help her pack and bring her back — and we must call in at Dave's on the way back, and try to get him to come to the funeral with us.' This seemed a sensible plan, and I agreed.

'We'll have to tell our families,' said Ann gently. 'I'll have to telephone my father, and you'll have to tell your brother and sister.'

'Yes,' I answered gloomily. It was a task I didn't relish, and I was still lost in reveries of my son.

Then Colin arrived; he was marvellous, saying little, but holding us close and identifying himself as much as he could with us in our great grief.

'I decided two things on the way over here,' he said. 'First, you are not to preach tomorrow, Douglas. Secondly you must go out for the funeral, and we'll help you to do so!'

We expressed our appreciation and remarked that we had reached similar conclusions. We told him that we planned to go and tell Maggie ourselves the next day, and call in on Dave on the way back. As I talked with Colin about tomorrow's sermon, Ann was trying to telephone Catherine at the cottage in Owen Sound. Eventually she got through.

'Hallo, Catherine dearest,' she said tenderly.

'Oh, Ma, this is so terrible,' she answered.

'Catherine dear, are you all right? Is there anyone with you?'

'Yes, there's a student here with me — and James.'

'Oh, good,' Ann replied.

'No, it's not good,' Catherine continued, and started to cry. 'A number of the students have been badly injured, and one has died.' She explained what had happened. Apparently as the minibus topped the brow of a hill, a swirl of snow blew into its path and sent it out of control. It headed straight into a truck coming towards it, and was badly smashed. Mike and a girl student sitting in the front were killed instantly. Two others were very badly injured and were taken by helicopter to hospital in Toronto. Four others were in the local hospital, and two were discharged with superficial injuries. But all were mentally and emotionally scarred for life. The police called it 'a freak weather accident'.

'What are *you* doing?' Ann asked, most concerned.

'I'm waiting for my parents to arrive, and they'll take me and James back to their place in Toronto.'

'We'll phone you tomorrow, Catherine,' said Ann, sensing that further talk was unrealistic. 'Goodbye, dear. All our love.'

It was good to have contacted Catherine; she was obviously still in a state of shock, but was evidently in good hands. We also had a first-hand account of the accident to digest later.

Colin decided he'd better write a sermon on his own rather than rely on my notes, and he needed to get back to prepare it. He prayed with us, committing us and our family — especially Catherine — to God's comfort and care and keeping; then he left.

We stirred ourselves into positive action; checking our diaries to see if we needed to cancel any appointments; checking our passports to see if they were still in date. Then I decided to telephone my sister; she is just eighteen months younger than I, and probably a little closer than my brother, seven years my junior. But I felt I must try to soften the bludgeon blow by breaking the news more gently than poor David had.

'Audrey,' I said, 'I'm afraid I've got some very sad news' (thus alerting her). 'It's Michael' (now she knew the person involved). 'He's been killed in a terrible road accident in Canada.' And as I spoke the words, the reality and the truth began to sink in upon me.

Audrey was upset and full of compassion and commiseration. We explained that we had briefly talked with Catherine, that we were all planning to go out to the funeral, with the church helping us out financially. We hoped that Dave would come too, but we didn't know at the moment when the funeral would be. She asked us to let her know our flight time and then she'd see us at the airport.

Sudden grief doesn't so much hit you as envelop you; a heavy lethargy, like a great grey blanket, wraps itself around you physically, mentally, emotionally, so that body, mind and feelings are all weighted down and oppressed. There were no tears; neither of us could cry, our emotions were too blanketed. Tears result from the release of emotion, not its suppression. But we were very heavy in our hearts.

The telephone rang and Ann answered it. It was Maggie. 'Hallo, dear,' she said brightly. They chatted pleasantries and swapped general news, Ann managing to keep her voice light and cheerful. Then Maggie said, 'A funny thing happened to me this afternoon.'

'What was that?' Ann asked with interest.

'Well, about two o'clock I suddenly burst into tears. It was convulsive crying, I couldn't stop. I've no idea why, but oh, it was awful. It took such hold of me. I don't know what caused it.' Ann expressed her sympathetic understanding, and then she asked Maggie her plans for Sunday, and learnt that after church in the morning she and a friend were going to the New Forest for lunch and a walk. After more chat she rang off.

'You were marvellous,' I said. 'How did you do it? You kept your voice bright and fresh. There was no trace of anxiety or worry at all. Marvellous!' and I kissed her. It was far better not to have told Maggie on the phone then, but to go and break the news to her in person the next day. Then Ann told me about Maggie's sobbing episode. We looked at each other and calculated the times; and we realized that dear Maggie had been overcome with crying at exactly the moment that Mike had died.

I had already phoned my sister. Now I must contact my brother before she did: I wanted to tell him myself. His wife Pippa answered and said that John wasn't in, but would be back in half an hour or so. 'I'll phone him later,' I said, 'unless he phones me when he comes in.'

'All right, Doug,' said Pippa, but sensing something was amiss, added, 'Is anything the matter?'

I hesitated: I could tell her, I suppose, but I'd prefer to

tell my own brother myself — he was also Mike's godfather. So I hedged. 'I'll talk to John about it,' I said simply.

Meanwhile Ann was trying to work out the times for our journey to Southampton tomorrow so that we would catch Maggie. After church she was going for a ramble with her flatmate, taking a sandwich lunch, so she wouldn't be going back to her flat. Ann decided to ring the vicar's wife, to tell her everything, and to suggest she ask Maggie back to the vicarage for coffee after morning service, and we would go straight there. There was no answer at first, and when eventually we did get through, it was to the vicar; his wife was away for the weekend. We told him, and explained that we would come down to Southampton to see Maggie ourselves; we'd get to the church when the family service ended, about 11.30 or so, and break it to her in the church.

The phone went again. Perhaps the need to communicate, the necessity of informing people and the contact with them on the telephone helped to lift the heavy blanket-pall of lethargy that had settled upon us both.

'Hallo,' I answered, in a voice I hardly recognized as my own.

'Douglas — it's Richard, Richard Third. Colin has just phoned to tell me your awful news. I'm so very sorry, so very sorry indeed. How is Ann?' It was our bishop speaking, full of concern and compassion.

'Ann's all right. It's a terrible blow, of course, and we keep thinking of his dear wife and baby son. We're planning to go out for the funeral.'

'Good,' he responded. 'I think that's important. I just want to assure you both of my love and prayers.'

'Thank you so much,' I replied. 'It was very good of you to phone.' A true pastor of his people is our bishop.

Two hours had gone by, and it was four hours since we'd eaten anything.

'I'll get something to eat', said Ann. 'What do you feel like?'

'Nothing,' I replied morosely, 'nothing to eat, just some

coffee.' So Ann got some coffee, and wisely added a few tit-bits to eat as well. We sipped our drink and nibbled our food in silence; there was nothing to animate either of us, nothing to say.

The phone rang. It was my brother.

'John,' I began, trying to get a grip on myself, 'I've got some very tragic news. It's Michael — he's been killed in a terrible road accident in Canada' — and now my voice was quaking as I knew I was convincing myself as well as infor-ming my brother.

He was shaken and, like any of us, did not know what to say. It's very difficult to know what to say when someone tells you his son has been killed. Words are quite inade-quate, and come out only as platitudes; sensitive compas-sion is all one can offer. He too felt so much for Catherine, and for baby James who, he added, 'will never know his father'. A chilling fact that hadn't got through to me until he spoke it. We did not talk for long.

Now Ann did her phoning. We were still anaesthetized with shock, so there were no tears, no choking voice. First she contacted her stepmother, and asked her to tell her elderly father (to whom it would come as a great shock) when she felt the moment opportune to do so. Then she phoned Maggie's fiancé Christopher, who was naturally quite choked. Chris was a curate (trainee minister) at a church near Peterborough, and due to take services the next day. He later told us that he very nearly broke down as he prayed for the bereaved at the morning service. Ann explained that we would be travelling to Southampton to tell Maggie in person, and to bring her back home; and that we all expected to go out to Canada for the funeral. Chris said he would probably get a couple of days off, and hoped to come to us on Monday to be with Maggie and comfort her.

We'd contacted everyone we needed to by then, and turned our thoughts to the next day: our journey to Southampton, calling at Reading to see David on our way back. We'd phone him from Maggie's at lunch-time to let him know when to expect us.

With leaden steps we climbed the stairs to our bedroom, and then into bed, where that very morning we had so enjoyed looking at the photographs of Mike and Catherine and their little son, who would now never know his father. The tears welled up as we thought of this, and we just hugged each other as they began to flow.

I felt aggrieved, but not devastated; I agonized, but wasn't distraught. Fatal accidents happen all over the world every day; now one had happened in our family and we must bear our great loss. We prayed together, especially for Catherine and James, and for the injured students. The light was out now, and I lay awake thinking of Michael. He had been the most difficult of our three children to bring up, with a strong will and a firm mind of his own. But he was never a rebel, always close to his family, and especially to his sister, just two years younger. In childhood she grew faster than he did and quite often they were mistaken for twins. This annoyed Michael who sent off (unbeknown to us) for a 'Bull-Worker' exercise kit to develop his muscles and, hopefully, to increase his stature. In his mid-teens he developed into normal height, with a good physique. He loved sport, especially rugger and tennis, enjoyed good food, and was very companionable, thus popular with guys and gals alike.

He didn't quite make it to Cambridge, his first choice, so he went to Durham, that loveliest of northern cities, where he played in the 2nds for rugger and the 4ths at hockey, sang in the college choir, supported the Christian Union, and generally enjoyed himself, the while working hard to get a good 2:1 degree in Geographical Sciences, just missing a first. His degree was good enough to get him a research scholarship at Carleton University in Ottawa. Immediately he was sent up to the North-west territories to study the geological effects of permafrost. He enjoyed this outdoor, adventurous life, which chimed in with his carefree spirit.

Back in Ottawa he threw his weight in with the Inter-Varsity Christian Fellowship (IVCF) and was asked to be chairman of the university branch in his final year. Here he met Catherine McColl who matched him in nature and temperament. He came home in the summer to look for a job and Catherine came soon after to meet us. We warmed to her at once; a lively personality, an ability to face life with a smile, and a positive Christian faith endeared her to us. So it was no surprise when, after their return to Ottawa, they announced their engagement. We were delighted, and began to save hard to go out to the wedding.

This took place the following summer in Toronto and a happy occasion it was. Maggie was a bridesmaid, and three of Mike's friends from Durham days came over, one to be best man and the other two to be ushers. Catherine was a hospital social worker in Ottawa and Mike had agreed to do a year at Ottawa University as staff worker for IVCF while finishing his thesis and doing some teaching at Carleton. After a year he tried unsuccessfully to get jobs in England, and when nothing materialized he accepted the position offered him by IVCF as the Southern Ontario staff director, based at McMaster University, Hamilton.

In the summer of '87 he and Catherine, then expecting a child, asked us to join them for their two-week holiday. How glad we are that we did — even though it meant selling some excess furniture to pay the fare — and how happy a time we had! We spent a week full of sunshine and lazy days at Grandad's Cottage at Owen Sound, and saw something of Mike's work at McMaster.

We travelled to the Pioneer campsite with him, and spent two happy, carefree days there. 'Pioneer' is a series of lakeside campsites owned and run by IVCF. Throughout the summer months groups of boys and girls, youngsters and teenagers, spend a fortnight there, supervised by Christian students who share their time, abilities, concern — and their faith. Mike was responsible for the pre-camp Leaders-in-Training Programme, a vital element in a well-structured set-up: over 2,000 youngsters attend the camps each summer, so leadership training is a key factor. It had been a glorious holiday; was it really only six months ago? We shall treasure those memories for the rest of our lives.

II

I slept fitfully and woke heavily. The pain of Mike's death stabbed me in the heart, and I groaned. The gloomy day loomed ahead: the day we would have to travel to break the sad news to Maggie.

We set off at nine o'clock for the journey to Southampton. It was a dull, grey day. We felt oppressed with the heavy lethargy of grief.

'How are we going to tell her?' I asked, naïvely. 'She'll be quite shocked to see us both.'

'I've been thinking of that,' Ann replied. 'I think it's best if I go first into church and find her, and you wait a few moments and then come.'

I didn't comprehend the logic of this; but I was too exhausted to argue, and decided to trust women's intuition.

We arrived at 11.20 and waited in the car near the church. After five minutes a few people began to emerge, but coffee was served after the service and there was a Christian bookstall open — both in the church itself. So the majority of the congregation were chatting inside, sipping coffee or browsing through books. We went to the porch and briefly spoke to the vicar. Then Maggie's flatmate saw us and raised her eyebrows enquiringly. Ann told her we had some very sad news for our daughter and she took her to find Maggie.

'Mum!' said Maggie in surprise. 'What are you doing here?'

'I have some very sad news,' Ann said gently.

'Is it Dad?' Maggie asked, not seeing me.

'No, darling, it's Michael.'

'Is he alive?'

Ann embraced her. 'No, dearest, he's not.'

They sat down together in a pew as I came up. Maggie burst into tears and sobbed her heart out.

'He wasn't just my brother,' she cried; 'He was my best friend.'

Two or three of her Christian friends gathered round, put their hands lightly on our shoulders, and prayed quietly, or silently for us. While our overwhelming grief went deep down inside each of us we knew, each one of us, an inner core of peace and tranquillity where God dwelt and was somehow mediating His presence to us.

After ten minutes or so we decided to go to Maggie's lodgings with Pat, her flatmate. Once there we told Maggie all we knew, and said we wanted her (and David) to come out to Canada for the funeral, which would probably be this very week. We allowed the tears to flow, to let out all the pent-up grief. We sobbed together, sharing in communion the emotion of the moment.

'There's no need to be ashamed of our tears,' I said, dabbing my eyes. 'In fact, it's best for our deep grief to work itself out in this way. We must express it somehow, and crying is the natural way.'

Once we'd composed ourselves, Maggie phoned the secretary of the school where she taught. Beryl was a friendly lady and a Christian who had 'mothered' her at the school. She came round and commiserated with us.

'Now you're not to think about school,' she said. 'I'll tell the headmistress, and we'll get your work covered for the next two weeks. You can ask for at least a week's compassionate leave, I know, in this case probably two — especially if you have to fly out to Canada.'

We were sipping coffee that Pat had thoughtfully provided, and it was obviously a relief to Maggie not to have to think about her school duties. Luckily she had marked all her books on Saturday, a chore she usually left to Sunday afternoons.

'I'll slip away now,' said Beryl, 'but before I go I'd like to say a prayer for you.' She held Maggie's hand and prayed deeply and realistically for God's peace and comfort for us all. 'Now I'll take your school books and you need not worry about it any more.'

We were grateful for her thoughtfulness and care for us. Pat brought in some more coffee — we were so dry — and some sandwiches. We munched and drank, not saying much.

Then Maggie said, 'I suppose I'd better go and pack, and see what warm clothing I've got for Canada.' Ann went to help her, while I phoned Dave to say we'd be with him about three o'clock. He was an hour's drive away.

We set off just before two o'clock and arrived at Dave's around three. He greeted us sombrely; fortunately his three-year-old elder son was out at a party and the younger, just 8 months, smiled uncomprehendingly at us all. We began at once to talk about the funeral arrangements. David had not been at Mike's wedding two and a half years earlier because of difficulty getting time off work and the considerable cost in both money and holiday time. Also, his wife Carolyn prefers not to fly, and disliked the idea of David flying. We realized this could be an obstacle, but felt sure Dave would want to be present at the funeral.

'David, we're going out to Toronto for the funeral, and Maggie's going to come too. The church has promised help with the fares. We very much want you to come. We'll help financially all we can, and I'm sure you'd get compassionate leave as . . . '

'It's all right, Mum,' Dave broke in, 'we've already decided. We've talked it over and Carolyn's happy for me to go. I'll get some days off work, and I'm owed a few anyway. And Uncle Derek's promised to help with the fare!'

Then poor Dave voiced his feelings; 'Why wasn't it me?' he cried out in a voice shaky with incomprehension. 'Why did I recover and Mike have to die?'

Ann soon put paid to that line of thought. 'Don't say

that, dear, nor even think it,' she said firmly. 'If you hadn't recovered, we'd have lost two sons.'

That, of course, was the only answer; but David, feeling almost guilty now that God had enabled him to recover, still found it hard to accept.

A car drew into the drive and my sister Audrey came in, followed by her husband Derek, a practising doctor. We embraced silently in turn. When words are inadequate, and known to be, gestures of affection and empathy are far more eloquent. Carolyn plied us with cups of tea, and Ann decided to try to phone Catherine at her parents' home in Toronto, to see if any funeral arrangements had yet been made. If the funeral was mid-week we might have to fly out the next day or the one after.

Audrey explained that they wouldn't be coming, but that her great Canadian friend, Pat, would be her representative at the funeral. Meanwhile Derek took me aside and gave me a cheque to help with David's fare.

'It's going to be pretty chilly in Canada,' said Derek. 'Have you got a warm coat, David?'

'Not really,' replied David with an embarrassed laugh, 'but I'll be all right.'

'Look,' said Derek, 'Take this. It's just the thing for a Canadian winter.' And he handed him his fur-lined leather coat. 'You can let me have it back sometime after you've returned.' With a grin David accepted his uncle's generous gesture.

Meanwhile Ann had at last got through to Catherine. She told her that all four of us would be flying out as soon as we could for the funeral. Catherine replied that she would be seeing to that on Monday, but it would probably be in Toronto about the middle of the week. She and James were bearing up well, she said, but she was concerned for the injured students. There was little more to say, and they rang off with expressions of mutual love and care.

It was time for departure. Audrey promised to come to the airport to see us off once we'd arranged our flight.

They drove off, we said our farewells, and drove through the dark back to Margate.

We called in on Ann's father and stepmother Pam at Birchington before going home. They provided us with welcome coffee and sandwiches, but Pa was very subdued. He was fond of his grandchildren, and had joined us in Canada on his own, two and a half years ago, for Mike's wedding in Toronto. Again, practical help was offered, Pam lending Ann her warm woolly jacket, and Pa giving me a cheque to help with fares and expenses.

As we entered our home, there were already six or eight letters on the door mat. Colin had announced Mike's death to a stunned congregation before the service had started that morning, and some had responded at once with cards and letters through the door. One letter told us that Colin had preached a most marvellous sermon, trying to come to terms with tragedy in the Christian life, but pointing us to the example of Christ, and the sure and certain hope in the resurrection that He gave all believers. We agreed; we knew that this was our strength and our hope, that this confidence in our faith was what kept us from falling apart.

We were so grateful for the support of our church family. When Mike became a full-time Christian worker, he had to find three-quarters of his salary himself. Our church undertook to provide a substantial part of that, and adopted him (and Catherine) as 'our own missionaries'. This involved persistent prayer support and regular financial support, and it meant a lot to them.

Colin himself called in about 9.30. He told us of the shock wave that had rippled back to him as he made the announcement, the gasps of 'Oh, no!' and the great compassion flowing out towards us. Then he handed us an envelope with love from the church family. Inside were three cheques; one made out to us for £1,000 to cover our air fares; the second for £500 made out to Catherine, and the third for the same amount, made out to Inter-Varsity Christian Fellowship, Mike's employers, for a memorial fund.

We were overwhelmed at such generous Christian caring. Within twenty-four hours of hearing of Mike's death we'd all been provided with our air fares to Canada!

Monday morning came and we drove into town to see about air tickets. We needed them in a hurry and we needed them cheap, two factors that did not easily go together. I was pleased to find a lady I knew behind the desk. I had taught her son, and we had met to discuss his progress and performance at parents' evenings. Her husband was a director of the agency.

'We need to fly to Toronto as soon as we can, please,' I began. 'There are four of us, but we'll need the cheapest fares possible.'

She read something in our faces. 'Can you tell me why you are going?' We explained it was for our son's funeral. She was full of concern, but it gave her an idea.

'I'll try Wardair,' she said, 'and explain the circumstances. They usually give a lower charge on compassionate grounds. I'll try them first.'

While she rang through, I picked up the Wardair brochure. There were flights most days except Tuesday; so it won't be tomorrow, I thought. Then I looked at the fares; if booked three weeks or more in advance, £333. If booked less than a week in advance £640: nearly double! Let's hope they can get the cheaper fare, I thought, there is over £1,200 difference! She couldn't get through, there was a half-hour delay, but she had booked a call. We decided to go to the bank and arrange for travellers cheques and Canadian money, and then come back.

She greeted us on our return: 'They have agreed to the lower cost, and you can fly on the Wednesday flight from Gatwick. If you give me details I'll prepare the tickets and you can collect them tomorrow.' We were greatly relieved, and we noted that the money we'd been given covered our four fares. Praise be!

Maggie and I went into the chemists next door to get a few things, and saw two parishioners; close friends both. But they turned away when they saw us, embarrassed, not knowing what to say. I don't blame them: death is *the* taboo subject in our present-day society. A society which has turned its back on God cannot face the mysteries of life and death. But for the Christian it should be different. I decided to go and speak with them, and in the end they were relieved, assuring us of their loving concern and caring prayers.

After a light lunch Maggie went upstairs to sleep, and Ann and I tried to rest. The phone went. It was Colin.

'Will you be in at four o'clock?' he asked.

'I expect so.'

'The Bishop wants to call in and see you. He's coming about four.'

'OK — thank you. We'll have a cup of tea ready.'

I told him we were flying out on Wednesday, though we didn't yet know when the funeral would be; but that the church's gift had exactly paid for three fairs, and I asked him to thank those concerned. Before ringing off, Colin told me he'd informed the Bishop, and also the Margate clergy with whom we met for a fraternal each month.

The doorbell rang. It was Eddie Rowlands, the Pentecostal minister, and his wife Heather. We all embraced.

'We had to come,' said Eddie, 'and see you both at this time.' We knew why; just over a year earlier Eddie and Heather had lost their son, a fine young man, in most distressing circumstances. Paul was about 21, and helped his dad in his ministry, especially working among young people. He had a flat of his own in Margate above the church premises. He suffered badly from asthma, and had a bad attack in his flat one morning; he was gasping, unable to breathe, choked himself, and was found dead — by his father — with his hand stretched out to the phone. Eddie rebuked himself for not phoning Paul before he left for the prayer meeting, but he also wondered why God hadn't nudged him at the meeting to go and see his son who so desperately needed him.

I had gone to Paul's memorial service, but it had bothered me a little: it was totally triumphalistic. Eddie had led it, and we'd sung songs of praise and victory. None of this was wrong, but there had been something missing and I had told Ann so afterwards.

'You know, Douglas,' Eddie said to me seriously, 'I've had to revise my theology. Yes, sir, I really have. Sure, Paul is in the Lord's hands and we can be thankful for that! But . . . .' he turned to look me full in the face, 'there is still an aching pain in the pit of the stomach. I've had to come to terms with that, Douglas and Ann, bless you! Maybe we've emphasized the victory of the cross, and rightly so, but we've not said enough about the pain and agony — that still lingers.'

I looked into his lined and drawn face, and we smiled sadly in our mutual grief over our sons. I was glad he had found what was missing in that service. Then he realized that he'd come not only to grieve with us, but also to comfort us. 'You know,' he said, 'chapter 11 of John's gospel is put there for a purpose. Yes, sir! You see when Lazarus died, his sisters Mary and Martha both said to Jesus: "If only . . . . If only you'd been here, Lord", but Jesus replied in effect, you're not to say "if only . . . ". Oh, Douglas,' Eddie went on, 'how often I've wanted to say "if only . . . " but then I've read John chapter 11 and it's been a great comfort; and I trust it will be to you, too.'

I was deeply grateful to this dear man for daring to bear his soul and his heartache to us at that time. But while the men reminisce, and wrestle with theology, the women in their practical way get on with the business of living. Heather produced a large bag which she handed over to Ann.

'I found one of the hardest things was to think of meals, and to go out shopping,' she said. 'So I've brought a bag of food, mostly basics really: bread, sugar, tea and so on. I thought it might be useful.' Ann was deeply appreciative. We embraced again in our common empathy and understanding before they left. Their visit had meant a lot to us.

The Bishop arrived just after four. 'I wanted to come and

see you myself,' he began. 'Now, tell me about your boy.' He got us talking about Michael naturally and positively, and we showed him a few of our photographs. As we sipped our tea, he suddenly said, '"Let nothing be wasted!" Our Lord's words, you know, at the feeding of the five thousand, "Let nothing be wasted". I'm quite, quite sure that nothing is wasted in God's service.' He paused and we let his words sink in. 'I'd like to believe that that thought may be a comfort to you.'

It was, and we knew it would be in the days to come. He prayed with us and for us, and for Catherine, and gave us his blessing before leaving. We felt truly blessed as God's servants had mediated His strength and His comfort to us in our hour of need.

That evening Chris, Maggie's fiancé, arrived and was a great support. We were exhausted and he was able to phone a few friends on our behalf. In addition he offered to drive us to Gatwick for the midday flight on Wednesday, which put our minds at rest.

Then Catherine phoned to say that the funeral had been arranged for 2.30 on Thursday in Toronto. It matched our flight well, as we would be arriving about 5pm on Wednesday evening and it would give us time to recover from the journey before the ordeal of the funeral.

Colin called in again and we gave him the details; he asked about the time differences and we told him five hours. 'Right,' he said, 'that fits in well. We will hold a little service and prayer time at St Mary's Chapel at 7.30 on Thursday to coincide with the service in Toronto. So many people have asked for some way to share in your grief and to support you. We'll hold this service at the same time, and we can all be remembering you and Catherine, and praying for you.' It was a fine gesture, which we much appreciated.

We then broached the subject of a memorial service here; there would be many family, friends and relatives who would want to remember Mike at a service in England.

Colin readily agreed to have it in Trinity church in a month's time: Saturday 13 February at 2.30. With date and time fixed, we could announce it in the obituary notice. Once he'd left, after a prayer with us, we began to compose the obituary.

A deep faith is undoubtedly the greatest strength in times of tragedy; to be able to communicate with God in prayer, to pour out one's heart to God and to *know* He not only hears, but shares our sorrow. Indeed, to be able to be angry with God, and even then to *know* He still understands. These are some of the fruits of faith. We have experienced in our anger, bewilderment, sorrow and grief the certain knowledge of the God who is there, caring for us, carrying us, sharing with us. The Psalmist knew this:

' . . . You hear, O Lord, the desire of the afflicted;
you encourage them, and you listen to their cry,
defending the fatherless and the oppressed, . . . '
Psalm 10, see verses 17, 18.

Again, the comfort of the Scriptures is another product of a personal faith. The Bible is considered by many to be largely irrelevant today, but in reality it is timeless in its application. It was a source of strength to us with David's illness; it was an equally strong support in Mike's death:

'For men are not cast off by the Lord for ever.
Though he brings grief, he will show compassion,
so great is his unfailing love.
For he does not willingly bring affliction
or grief to the children of men.'
Lamentations 3:31-33.

Above all, the twin pillars of Christianity — the incarnation and resurrection of Jesus — are the strongest supports of all. To know that Christ is with us in our grief, and shares in it because he was born into humanity as a divine human being, means that 'the peace which passes all understanding' dwells deep in our hearts; and to know that death is not oblivion, not the end, but merely a stepping-stone to the resurrection; to *know* these twin truths is to be able to walk firmly in the midst of personal tragedy: 'Though I walk through the valley of the shadow of death, *thou art with me*'.

In addition the man or woman of faith will be a member of a worshipping community: 'the company of all believers', who share the same beliefs, and who will provide support — both spiritual and practical — in times of need.

We received letters and cards from parishoners and friends, acquaintances and relatives. One or two enclosed a cheque to help out with personal expenses, all sent messages that were heart-felt. One of the most moving was from a woman with profound personal problems, whom Ann and I had each counselled over the years. She wrote just eight words in her own hand, and it meant a lot to us: 'I love you — and I'm hurting with you.' That said it all.

Wednesday came, a bleak day, reflecting our feelings. But there wasn't much time for feelings as we had to set off early for the airport. Both Ann and I had only slept fitfully, and were so relieved to leave the driving to Chris. A package of mail arrived just as we set off, and we opened the letters in the car. We were very touched by so many expressions of support and sympathy.

One thoughtful, positive letter from a Christian couple read, 'We know that your faith in God will shine undimmed in the darkness of sorrow, and that He will be your strength . . . God used Colin today as, in shock, we, your family in Christ, were told that we must stand firm in our relationship of belief and trust in God. To our question of "Why?" there is no answer. To our question "where is God?" the answer is that He is with us . . . He is suffering with us, He really knows what we feel. Because of Mike's death, both Colin's sermons were outstanding in their reasoning and reassurance. Many such sermons will be preached by devoted servants of God because of Mike's death. Many seeking God will find Him. Many will be strengthened in their faith, find unity with each other, and a deeper understanding of the meaning of being a

Christian. May God grant you both and all your dear ones here and in Canada His peace and His strength in all your ways.'

We found this heart-warming and truly Christian. If the darkest hour in the world's history was when men murdered God and nailed Him to a cross, the brightest day dawned with the resurrection that sprang from that awful act, a resurrection that gave new life, new hope and victory over empty death. This is the meaning of our faith, and this letter had affirmed it . . . 'Because of Mike's death, many seeking God will find Him . . . .' This was our hope, our prayer, and our firm conviction.

At the airport we met my sister Audrey, who had gone to Reading to collect David, thus saving his children and Carolyn the depressing experience of an airport farewell. Instead, they would come and meet him on his return. We said our goodbyes to Audrey and Chris and climbed on board. I lay back and reflected. Here we were, off to Canada again, but this time without any of the anticipation or excitement of our previous visits. Instead, our hearts were leaden; flying out for the worst possible reason — to bury Michael. Or rather, to bury his body. His Lord, whom he had loved and served, would take over from here, and his life would ever be a bright memory for us. This was what so underlined the tragedy for us. Not only was Mike a 'great all-round chap to have around', he loved life and lived it to the full. He ran towards life with his arms wide open and a smile on his face, taking into himself all the good experiences that came his way. He'd climbed up Mount Sinai at 2am to watch the dawn in the desert; he'd flown over the Yukon sea to watch the sunset in the Arctic. He'd acted in Rogers' 'Oklahoma', and sung in Brahms' 'Requiem'. He'd hitch-hiked over much of Europe and piloted a glider over England. He'd walked from Bath to Wells as a boy and driven from Ottawa to Alaska as a man. And all the time he'd been faithful to, and witnessed to, his Lord and Master.

'Ah, sweet mystery of life,' sang the poet — and there is a mystery about life, about its creation and its procreation. But I say, 'Oh, deep mystery of death' — a more profound mystery which no one can penetrate. The death of a child or a young person throws it into relief; Why? Why? And there is no answer, only an echo. Somebody once said, 'Nobody should ever have to go to their own child's funeral' — again highlighting the mystery. I have visited old people in their nineties, 'cabin'd, cribb'd and confined', longing for death and release from a wasted body racked with pain. Death will certainly come to each one of us we know (though many find that hard to accept), but why it comes so early to some and so late to others is a profound mystery.

'I'm just wondering how I shall greet Catherine,' Ann broke in on my thoughts. 'It is important we say the right words when we meet her. I'm going to pray about this.' She closed her eyes and talked to her Lord. I marvelled at my wife. Here was I, thinking only of our great loss. There was she, thinking only of other people and linking them to God. She lived out her Christian faith more than I did.

It was a boring, uneventful flight; I usually seized the opportunity of long hours sitting down to catch up with my reading, but I couldn't concentrate enough to read, so dozed intermittently. The plane was late arriving and it was after six in the evening when we landed (having put our watches back five hours). As soon as we emerged we saw Catherine with her Dad, George, alongside her, looking trim and composed, though with sorrow and slight apprehension in her eyes. Ann threw her arms around her.

'You're as precious as our daughter, and always will be, and we love you so much!' She spoke from the heart; this wasn't the time for pleasantries or pretence. They just wept on each other's shoulders, hugging each other tight, the wife and the mother bonded in a common grief.

By the time Maggie and David and I had embraced Catherine and George, he was looking agitated. 'I'm parked where I shouldn't be,' he said, 'so the sooner we pack your bags in the car and get going the better.'

The six of us with all our baggage packed into the one car, and travelled through the dusk to Catherine's parents' home. There was a meal awaiting us, but we were too tired to eat much.

There, however, we found baby James, and we took him into our arms and held him tightly. He was very precious and meant even more to us now. Our eyes welled with tears, tears of pride at holding Mike's son, tears of pain at knowing how much he wanted to show him to us himself.

'Dr Baxter's coming along soon,' said Catherine. 'He's giving the funeral oration tomorrow.' We remembered that he had preached at Mike and Catherine's wedding thirty months earlier. 'He said he'd like to call in and see us, and talk over one or two things. He's been marvellous,' she added, 'so helpful to us all.'

When he arrived he greeted us warmly yet sombrely. He explained that we'd be going to the mortuary in the morning as Catherine was very anxious to see Mike's body, to say her final farewell. However, he was concerned for her, as Mike had been so severely damaged. Nevertheless, we would meet there at half past ten, and we agreed to accompany Catherine.

'Now, Douglas,' he turned to me. 'Would you like to read the Scriptures or lead the prayers tomorrow at the service?'

I hesitated; I had plenty of experience of doing both, but would I be up to doing so at my own son's funeral, I wondered. Yet it would be a positive Christian witness if I could.

'Yes,' I said, 'I'll read the lesson. Do you know what it is?'

'You can choose it yourself,' he replied; 'Though I'd like you to include the verses at the end of 1 Corinthians 15: "When the perishable has been clothed with the imperishable, and the mortal with immortality", if you will. But you know the Scriptures, so you choose what you wish.' I consented, but it occupied my mind considerably as I went to bed.

A cold, grey light filtering through the curtained window awoke me. Where was I, what was I doing in this unfamiliar room? Gradually the truth dawned as the light grew brighter. I was in Canada and today I was going to bury my dearly-beloved son. I felt cold and grey inside, matching the wintry weather outside. Suddenly the anger, frustration, emotion and heartache welled up inside me and I broke into deep sobbing. I buried my face in my pillow so as not to wake Ann, but heard her quietly sobbing too. Somehow we both felt better for it; all the pent-up emotion of the last four days was released, and it worked its own therapy.

'There's no need to be ashamed of our tears,' I said softly, repeating the words I'd spoken in Maggie's flat last Sunday morning. 'No need at all. Jesus wept when His best friend died, and I'm not ashamed of crying.'

I reached out for my bedside Bible and read through Paul's great chapter on the resurrection (1 Corinthians 15). Yes, I thought, I'll read some of this at the funeral, but there's something else I must read as well.

Downstairs George was fixing breakfast for us. We weren't hungry, just thirsty, and drank and drank tea or coffee to dampen the awful dryness in the mouth. Then it was time to face the mortuary.

Apparently it is the Canadian custom for the deceased to be displayed in an open coffin a day or so before the funeral. The closest relatives would be seated at the head, and mourners would visit the mortuary to pay their respects to the deceased, and to show their sympathy with the relatives. It was a prospect that had no appeal at all to any of us, and we were so glad that the McColls had cancelled this empty custom, not only out of consideration for our feelings, nor just because of Mike's battered condition. They recognized the hollowness of a custom in which the grief-stricken family are unduly over-taxed, and the mourners can mostly mouth shallow sentiments.

The mortuary was a plush building, pile-carpeted and with deep settees. We were met there by Dr Baxter and Don Posterski, the Ontario director of IVCF and Mike's boss, who was to conduct the service. Both were sombre-suited and grave of face. Dr Baxter took Catherine aside and Don spoke to us.

'We're trying to persuade Catherine not to view Mike's body; it can only upset her. We've been ourselves, and although the morticians have done what they could, he's barely recognizable.'

'Barely recognizable'; the words hit me in the pit of my stomach and I felt sick. Handsome, fair-haired Mike, with open smiling face and bright shining eyes, 'barely recognizable'. I groaned inwardly as we seated ourselves heavily in the foyer.

Soon Catherine emerged with eyes full of tears yet resolve on her face. She had desperately wanted to say her own personal farewell to her beloved Michael, just to kiss him goodbye. His death four days ago had been so sudden, and such a numbing shock, that she needed the reality to sink in. Viewing his body would help this process — and also confirm the nagging doubt we all have that there had been some mistake, that they'd got the wrong person. So she was quite naturally upset when Dr Baxter advised against viewing his battered body and fractured face, and she sobbed her heart out on his broad compassionate shoulders. But once she'd got control of her emotions she agreed that it was far better to remember Mike as he was, as he had been in life, than to view his damaged husk in death. But it hurt, it hurt terribly, and it hurt deep, deep down.

Her mother, aware of the pain, came across and made a suggestion: if the face was covered over, and the lights dimmed, then Catherine could go in, take Mike's hand in hers and remove the wedding ring. This was readily agreed, and Posterski went to arrange it. He returned and softly informed us that the top half of the body was now covered with a sheet and the light directed on his hand. Catherine braced herself resolutely.

'I'd like to go in alone,' she said simply. But her parents and Dr Baxter accompanied her to the door of the mortuary, and waited there for her return. We watched heavy-hearted as the four of them walked slowly away.

We sat and waited, and prayed silently for strength for Catherine: spiritual and physical strength, that is; she had already proved her great strength of character. The time dragged, but it was probably only three minutes before they returned, Catherine with a proud, contented smile on her tear-lined face. I felt proud of her, too: it must have been an ordeal, but she'd done what she felt she needed to do, and we all respected her for that.

'Would you like us to serve you some coffee?' the supervisor asked. We dithered. We'd all been so caught up in the emotion of the moment that even a restful respite seemed an intrusion.

Catherine quickly decided. 'No,' she said firmly. 'No, thank you! Let's go from this place; we can all relax and have coffee at home.' And she led the way out.

Don Posterski joined us for coffee back home, and spoke briefly about the arrangements for the service. As he left he handed me a copy of the specially-prepared funeral leaflet. There was a head-and-shoulders picture of Mike on the front and underneath: MICHAEL JOHN HARE: 17 MAY 1960 – 16 JANUARY 1988. At that moment a lead weight hit my stomach and I knew for a certainty that Mike was dead, dead and gone forever. There was his birth date, and there was his death date. His span of life on earth was firmly and finally and irrevocably fixed, proclaimed, announced to all the world. I went upstairs, ostensibly to prepare for my reading at the funeral service, but first I sobbed my heart out for my son. Then I looked at the reading on my knees.

Joan McColl had produced just the right lunch for the sombre occasion; sandwiches, celery, sausage rolls and the like to help ourselves to, buffet-style. Catherine's brothers and their wives arrived, and her sister from the States. David was asked to be a pallbearer, and readily agreed. I looked at Catherine; my heart went out to her, and it swelled with pride, too. She looked trim and neat in a cream suit without a trace of doleful black. 'That's right, girl,' I thought. 'Even mourning can — and should — be positive for the Christian!'

Eddie Rowlands's words came back to me: 'The pain in the pit of the stomach is still there!' Of course it is, and it's foolish to deny it. But so is the victory, the blessed hope of the resurrection life, and it is right to affirm it! Catherine was affirming it, though the pain would be greater for her than for any of us.

The family cars moved off and Catherine's father George drove us in his big Buick to the church. When we arrived I gasped, for the large car park was crowded, but George managed to manoeuvre into a reserved plot. I heaved a big sigh; the last time we'd come here was a bright, sunny, August day for Mike's wedding. Now we'd come on a dull, chilly, January day for his funeral. The contrast hit home. We were ushered by a side door into the ministers' vestry where church officials and Don Posterski greeted us quietly, assuring us that seats were reserved at the front where we'd go in just before the service started. A short prayer together and we filed in.

The large modern Baptist church was packed tight, so much so that there was an overspill of the congregation assigned to chairs on the dais, behind the minister's lectern, sitting rather embarrassingly facing us. As we took our seats, we saw them before we saw the coffin, perched on a wheeled trolley below the minister's desk, about waist-level, so that one looked over it to the speaker, and to the cross above and behind him. How much better, I thought, than the British way, where the coffin is placed at eye-level and totally dominates the service.

The opening sentences over, I moved forward tensely to the rostrum, praying that the Lord would give me a strong voice that did not quake or quaver. I looked out on the congregation and began to speak so naturally the opening verse (which I knew) that the congregation were startled, believing I was addressing them rather than reading the Scriptures:

'Someone may ask, "How are the dead raised? With what kind of body will they come?" How foolish! What you sow does not come to life unless it dies . . . ' and I read on through the Apostle Paul's great chapter on the resurrection. (1 Corinthians 15:35.) Then I switched to Romans 8: 'What, then, shall we say in response to this?' I asked in a matter-of-fact voice: 'If God is for us, who can be against us? . . . . For I am convinced that neither *death*, (and I paused for emphasis), nor life, neither angels nor demons, neither the present nor the future, nor any powers, neither height nor depth, nor anything else in all creation, will be able to separate us — or Michael — from the love of God that is in Christ Jesus our Lord.' God had heard my prayer, for my voice had been as strong at the end as at the start; and I'd been enabled to make my own personal insertion into Paul's majestic words.

The tension relaxed as we all stood to sing a hymn. Catherine had bravely chosen one which had been sung at their wedding two and a half years earlier, 'We rest on Thee, our shield and our defender'. As we sang, a tall man slipped to the front and onto the dais; we recognized John Bowen, Mike's great friend from Ottawa, who'd encouraged him to join the IVCF staff. The hymn over, Don Posterski spoke warmly of Mike, of his great promise, of his leadership qualities, chief of which was his willingness to serve others, and of his natural friendly nature which endeared him to so many.

John Bowen then led the prayers in a conversational tone addressing his heavenly Father, unafraid to express his bewilderment, even his anger, at the tragic event. 'Father,' he went on, 'where were your love and your power when we needed them? Like the psalmist we feel like asking you why you were sleeping instead of looking after your people. But Jesus shows us that you are a God who does not reject us when we are angry or confused. Thank you that we are invited to bring our confusion and our doubts, our anger and our pain to you, knowing that you will welcome us . . . . Jesus has shown us that you are a God who weeps over death and is angry at evil. We know that you lost your special Son through a violent death. As we mourn, may we know your presence as very real, weeping and feeling the pain as we do.'

He went on to pray that some good may come from this evil, that we will see in the months and years ahead some fruit from Mike's death; that our commitment to Christ may be deepened. He prayed for specific people, beginning with Catherine and James, Mike's family, for the family of the student killed; he prayed for all the injured students, their families and friends. And he ended: 'Thank you for the historical reality of Jesus' resurrection . . . . And help us to live every day in the light of this "eternal perspective" that we are so conscious of right now.' It was a deep-felt prayer, so real, and most moving.

Dr Baxter then preached on the Christian hope, linking it to our journey through life, emphasizing Departure and Destination. The service concluded with the singing of one of Mike's favourite hymns, 'The day Thou gavest, Lord, is ended'.

Catherine's three brothers, our David, and two close student friends from McMaster accompanied the coffin as it was wheeled down the central aisle (rather than borne aloft on strong shoulders), and the immediate family filed out behind it. At the doorway Catherine turned to me and said, 'That was the finest service I've ever been at!'

I smile at her: 'Except your marriage service, my dear,' I thought, but did not say it aloud. She told me later that she meant it, and still means it. Whereas the wedding had been wonderful and very special, Mike's funeral had been especially meaningful. It had been inspiring and uplifting; indeed, she then first began to feel the deep healing of that raw open wound which sudden bereavement incurs. The service was totally real. It was not just a ceremony to be got through. For it acknowledged and faced the grief but also portrayed the great resurrection hope of eternity with Jesus.

If the service was the finest, the burial was a fiasco. Catherine had purchased a plot in a private cemetery not far away. The hearse was ready, the funeral car with relatives behind it; George had our family in his car. But there was some confusion and the cortège did not move off for about ten minutes. Eventually we set out; snow was swirling, blown about by an icy wind. The drive was short; only about eight minutes, and the three cars came to a halt. But there was no minister to conduct the committal, no pallbearers to carry the coffin. The young funeral director was perplexed, and so were we. It seems that someone had dismissed them, unbeknown to us. The bewildered director approached us: 'I'm afraid I'll have to ask you three gentlemen to help us with the coffin,' he said apologetically. 'I've only two men here and . . . ' he raised his hands helplessly.

So David, George and I helped his staff to lift out the coffin and carry it to the graveside. The gravity of the situation kept my anger in check; but I felt then, and still do today, that I should never have been asked to carry my own son's coffin — nor should David, his brother — from the hearse to the grave. In fact, it was so remote that unreality took over, the swirling wind and bitter snow, frozen feet trudging the icy ground; carrying a corpse to a gaping hole; it was all a bad dream, totally divorced from life, from reality.

We reached the grave and I jerked myself back to find it was real, all too real. We placed the coffin on two planks across the grave and I stepped back, waiting for the act of committal and the lowering of the coffin into the grave. The rest of the family had joined us. Should I say a prayer myself, as a Christian pastor, albeit a layman? I did not know the words of committal, so we all bowed our heads in silent prayer. Apparently there'd been a misunderstanding about the arrangements and so Dr Baxter had pronounced the words of committal at the end of the church service: 'Dust to dust, ashes to ashes . . . .' Catherine bravely stepped forward and placed a rose on the coffin as she said aloud, 'Goodbye, my love.'

I looked for the ropes to lower the coffin into the grave, which I assumed was our next job, but the funeral director and his men were already walking away, and so we followed. Seated in the warmth of the car I looked out at the ridiculous scene, and unreality took over again. There was Mike's coffin perched on a plank on top of the grave, in the middle of this park; the headstones were all flat at ground level, so the coffin stood out prominently. The bleak day, the leaden sky, the few flakes of snow falling and blowing in the icy wind — I felt I was taking part in a bizarre scene in a Fellini movie, acting out a role; this couldn't be *real!* We drove off leaving the coffin incongruously alone in the middle of the meadow.

Others shared my disbelief at this extraordinary scene. Catherine and Maggie were actually able to chuckle, imagining what Mike might have said: 'Cor, what wallies! You might have done the job properly and finished it off!'

Back at the church we realized that many of the congregation had waited in a hall the half-hour we were away in order to express their sympathy with us; now we needed to go and meet them. But the ladies wanted to compose themselves and tidy their hair first, so we went into an adjacent side-room. However, some saw us and stood at the doorway. There at the front I saw my dear friend Bill Draper and his wife Pat. We'd known each other since we were teenagers in the Scouts together. I realized that they knew no one else here, only us; so I went across to greet them. As

I did so a little Chinese lady pushed her way in front: 'Mr Hare,' she said quickly, 'I'm Mrs Lee; and this is my son Andrew. He's a student at McMaster, *and he was in the accident!*' I looked at the young man, rather bewildered with a strained face bearing a bruise.

'Andrew,' I said warmly, 'how glad I am to meet you!' And I shook his hand encouragingly. 'Thank you very much for coming — it's good of you to be with us today.' I hadn't had time to think of what to say; I felt God's Spirit guided me. Bill and Pat embraced Ann and me, conscious that words could not convey deep feelings. I thanked them for coming, and they asked how long we were there for, and promised to keep in touch.

Then into the crowded hall. The chatter became more subdued as we entered, and soon each of us was surrounded by a small group of people anxious to convey their condolences. A tall professor of theology came up to me with tears streaming down his face. 'Oh, Mr Hare,' he said. 'This is a terrible tragedy!' His wife embraced Ann silently. He taught at McMaster, and they were great supporters of IVCF and of Mike personally. We'd met them just six months earlier when Mike had asked them to join us for a barbecue in the garden. Now they were broken-hearted, and shared our grief. We were deeply touched and our tears flowed too. Students came and, with sad faces, silently shook our hands. One slightly-built girl said simply, 'Thank you for your reading of the Scriptures.' One or two others said how much the Scripture reading had meant to them.

Another group gathered round, and I recognized the pastor from the church in Ottawa which Mike and Catherine used to attend. I was stunned; this man had travelled over 300 miles — a six-hour journey each way — to come to Mike's funeral, and had brought a few friends with him. We chatted together, then we saw Thea, also from Ottawa, who'd been like a mother to Mike when he had first arrived there, and with whom we stayed whenever we visited. She and Ann both wept on each others' shoulders; grief must have its say.

Still people came — close friends and distant strangers — some with tears and some with sad smiles, but all anxious not just to support us in our grief but to share it with us. Another very close friend of Mike's, a student pastor at his church, with whom we'd lunched during our summer holiday, was overwhelmed with sobs and couldn't say a thing; yet his young wife was able to talk with Ann. A middle-aged well-groomed man shook my hands warmly and introduced himself in a Scottish accent, 'I'm a geography professor from Carleton (Ottawa again; where Mike did his MA thesis) and I have a letter here. I'm glad to be able to give it to you in person. Open it at your leisure when you've more time to consider it. I'm so pleased to have been here today.' I thanked him for coming such a distance for such a sad occasion as he handed me a sealed envelope from Carleton University.

Meanwhile his colleague was speaking to Ann. He'd been instrumental in inviting Mike to Canada straight from Durham, and Mike had assisted him in some research. He'd also been Mike's supervising professor for his thesis, and Mike had got on well with him. We'd dined with them when we first went out to Canada. He respected Mike's Christian stance without being so inclined himself.

'Thank you so much,' said Ann, 'for all you did for Mike.' He looked at her, 'It's not half as much as he did for me', he replied, and his eyes filled with tears.

A young man approached us. 'Hello,' he said, 'I was involved in the research project with Mike up in Yukon. We shared a lot together, all sorts of experiences. I've got some photographs of that time and I've put them all in a special album. Now,' he went on, 'when James is somewhat older, say a little boy, I want to show him those photographs, tell him what fun we had together, and what a super guy his Dad was!'

Again we were overwhelmed. Professors and students,

colleagues and co-workers, Mike had won the respect of each and everyone. Although no one speaks ill of the recent dead, especially those who die young, what was it that drew so many diverse people to honour Mike by attending his funeral? Perhaps he was one of those rare people whose 'life was gentle and the elements so mixed in him' in the right proportions, to give a harmony, a balance; a cheerful manner, yet a serious nature; a firm faith, yet an enquiring mind; a love of life, yet a love for his Lord; thoughtful yet outgoing; considerate yet reckless; daring yet cautious; open yet committed. These traits most of us have, yet one is usually dominant. In Mike they blended, seemingly without conflict, but in 'perfect harmony'. Maybe this was why he could relate so easily and happily to so many different people.

Suddenly Catherine turned to us, a smile on her strained face. 'One thing I've definitely decided,' she said perkily, 'I'm still coming over for Maggie's wedding in May!' and she embraced her sister-in-law. It was a marvellous, positive gesture at the end of a gruelling day.

Friday was an anticlimax, with nothing to occupy mind or body, no fixed points of time to work towards. Don Posterski came round about mid-morning, and we thanked him warmly for yesterday's service. 'There's this service at Hamilton on Sunday,' he said. 'Now this is a memorial service, not a funeral. So it's got to be different.'

We agreed whole-heartedly. 'I'm thinking of three or four different people all saying a few words about Mike; how does that seem to you?'

'Yes,' I responded; 'but it's important it is just a *few* words. We don't want three or four people each giving fifteen-minute eulogies.'

'Quite right!' he affirmed. 'In fact, I'm going to limit them to three or four minutes each.'

'That's fine!' I agreed.

'So, Doug,' he went on, 'how would you like to speak on family memories?' I smiled ruefully; having insisted that each memory was a brief one I was now being asked to encapsulate twenty-seven years of family memories of Mike into three or four minutes — an impossible task. I stalled for time. 'I'll think about it,' I said.

'Well,' said Don, 'We'll need to know by nine o'clock tomorrow morning in order to print out the service. You'll be sure to let us know by then, won't you?' I promised I would.

I awoke early and lay awake, thinking that I'd soon have to answer Don's suggestion for family memories. Sure we had some: they'd take an hour or more to tell. I looked across at Ann just waking; and suddenly I had an idea and I knew it was right. I slipped across and climbed into bed with her. 'Those family memories Don's asked me to do,' I said. 'Would you be able to do some with me? Could we share it together?' She smiled. 'I wondered if you were going to ask me,' she replied, 'because I thought I would like to share it with you. It would be nice to do it together.'

'Do you think you'll be able to?' I asked, concerned.

'Yes, I'd like to.'

'Right,' I said. 'I'll phone Don and say we'll do a joint effort.' Also I thought that as there were two of us, that would give us seven minutes! During the morning we worked it out: we each had two anecdotes of Mike as a boy, and each story revealed something of Mike's character as a man; so it should be appropriate.

The Drapers came to collect us for lunch and drove us out to an old-fashioned restaurant they knew in north Toronto. We loved them dearly, but somehow it wasn't a success. They didn't know what to say and we weren't into pleasantries or idle chit-chat. The numbness of the week-old news was wearing off and our sense of loss, deep, deep loss, was beginning to overwhelm us. I felt as if I'd had a limb amputated. David and Maggie said little, and we soon tired of table talk.

The raw wound of our loss was being exposed to the chill air of the 'real' world and it hurt, really hurt, deep down. I couldn't reconcile my inner world, enveloped in pain and grief, with the everyday normality outside. My head was bursting and I wanted to shout out loud: 'Why are you chatting and laughing? Why are you buying and selling? Why are you carrying on as if nothing has happened? Haven't you heard the terrible news? My son is dead. My son is dead!'

C. S. Lewis describes grief as very similar to fear. I suppose he means in the way it can overwhelm you, can totally envelop you, affecting you mentally, physically, emotionally, the way it can gnaw its ghastly presence into your very soul. If that soul is empty the result is devastation; but if God dwells in that soul, both fear and grief are rebuffed and are gradually overcome by His pervading peace.

The Drapers drove us back to the McColls, as we had an important engagement at half past three. We said our farewells and they departed, while we took ourselves in hand for the next business. It could prove to be something of an ordeal.

Catherine was determined to visit the badly-injured students who had been transferred to a specialist hospital unit in Toronto. Dr Baxter, who was chaplain to the hospital, was coming to collect her, and we offered to go along with her as well.

The sky was low and dreary as we drove to Sunnybrook Hospital and found our way to the specialist unit on the fifth floor. We enquired after Geraldine, the most seriously injured girl, and were ushered into a waiting-room. There was a tall, grey-faced man already there, and Dr Baxter greeted him and introduced us. He was Geraldine's father and also a physician at the hospital. He commiserated with us over our loss, and expressed his deep concern over his daughter ever walking again. My heavy heart went out to him. I recalled my own son David in intensive care ten years earlier: the awful waiting, the wounding wondering, the mental wrestling, the agony of not knowing, the whole long, strong, painful process. It was a sad meeting.

Eventually we were allowed in briefly to see Geraldine; she was (not unnaturally) upset at meeting Catherine, but much appreciated our visit. We encouraged her all we could.

Our spirits were low and dreary as we drove away under a lowering sky, now spitting out icy rain or snow. All we could think of was the awful tragedy of it all, just a week ago now. 'The essence of tragedy,' wrote the Shakespearean scholar A. C. Bradley, 'is waste.' Two young people dead, two seriously injured, four others badly hurt, all scarred for life. A totally unnecessary waste of human life and limb — what a tragedy indeed!

Sunday dawned, dull, grey and lifeless. The memorial service was at Mike and Catherine's home church in Hamilton, an hour's drive away, and was due to start at 2.30. George drove Ann and me to the church, and there we composed ourselves in a side-room and looked at the service sheet.

Don had done his job well. He'd involved the minister of the church and the chairman of Hamilton IVCF Area Committee, Dorothy Pinnock. In addition to ourselves, 'Memories of Mike' were to be given by the student president of McMaster IVCF, Professor Clarke Pinnock of the Divinity School, Mike's great friend Jeff Kingswood, and the general director of IVCF Canada. I hoped each would keep to his or her allotted time of three to four minutes. There was a main address to be given by John Bowen. Interspersed were a couple of violin solos by a professional musician, which particularly pleased Catherine. We were praying for the injured, and praying responsively too, and we were to conclude with a great chorus of affirmation: 'Jesus is Lord!' On the back of the service sheet Don had arranged for this to be printed:

> Mike's life spoke the words written by his favourite Christian author, John Stott.
>
> 'Don't be content with the mediocre! Don't settle for

anything less than your full God-given potential! Be
ambitious and adventurous for God! God has made you
a unique person by your genetic endowment, upbring-
ing and education. He has Himself created and gifted
you and He does not want His work to be wasted. . . .
His purpose is that everything you have and are should
be stretched in His service and in the service of others.'

It was a fine tribute and we felt very proud.

We took our seats near the front, and the rest of the
family soon arrived. Just before the service started, a large
man came slowly down the aisle with his wife; looking
somewhat bewildered they sat down heavily in the front
row. Afterwards we learnt that they were the German-born
parents of the young girl student who had been killed in
the accident, and that the wife spoke no English. At the
end of the service we went up and silently embraced them,
united in grief. Then we thanked them warmly for sharing
in this service with us only a day or so after burying their
own daughter. We were very touched by their brave and
loving tribute.

The church was packed. Somewhere around four hundred people were present. The service proceeded as
planned and took on its own unique character. There was
humour as well as sadness, praise as well as prayer. The
tributes were pertinent and brief, the violin solos providing
just the right atmosphere. John Bowen spoke brilliantly on
John 12:20-28: '"Unless an ear of wheat falls to the ground
and dies it remains only a single seed. But if it dies, it
produces many seeds."' He paid glowing tribute to Mike,
but all the while pointed us to Jesus, whom Mike loved and
served. We were able to recount our anecdotes, too, and
draw a lesson from each little story.

Somehow our light-hearted approach relieved the tension; and it was a glorious freedom to be able to be light
of heart — yet this reflected Mike so well. He laughed
at life, and chuckled his way through life; yet he was never

superficial or shoddy. John Bowen had told how Mike had continued at Carleton University as an associate staff worker for a pittance, whereas students he'd been teaching were getting jobs at three or four times his salary. Questioned incredulously about this, Mike had replied with his disarming smile: 'You're not going to change the world without making some sacrifices!'

Why were we able to be light-hearted in the midst of a solemn service? This should have been the saddest occasion in our life, now that the stunned numbness of the event was wearing off. Partly it was because memories of Mike always brought a smile, but only partly. Two further factors, closely related, came into play.

The first was simply that for us Mike was alive: alive in our memories, alive as part of our lives. And those who lose loved ones — and we all do — need to hold fast to those living memories, those happy times shared, the life together. Gloomy grief takes over when we look back selfishly and long wistfully for former joys. This way leads to pain and sorrow, for it is no use living in the past, as if the present doesn't exist, or at least doesn't matter. Grief is there with us and always will be. The physical equivalent of losing a loved one is having one's arm or leg amputated at its base. A part of *you* is missing, and always will be. It's no good looking back to when you had your limb; you have to manage now without it. So we need to face each day positively, aware of our loss, of course, but aware too that life has to be lived in the present. So Mike was alive for us, and always would be, and we would talk about him and talk to others about him just because he was — is — part of our life today.

The second reason we could look up with a smile on such a sad day was our Christian hope of the resurrection. 'Hope' is almost too weak a word; conviction — even certainty — might be better. 'If only for this life we have hope in Christ, we are to be pitied more than all men,' wrote Paul. We know that because Christ rose from the dead, then all who die 'in Christ' will also enjoy the resurrection life. This is not a pious hope (in the sense of 'I hope so'); it is a foundation of the Christian faith tested and proved over 2,000 years. True, and a truth we can hold on to. But the arm is still amputated; there's still the pain in the pit of the stomach.

Towards the end of the service Don expressed these ideas in his own way. 'This service has reminded us that in the Christian understanding of life somehow, out of death comes life. So we go from this place looking for shafts of light to continue to come out of the pain and horror of this last week . . . .' He mentioned receiving a letter two days ago from a student saying that on reflecting on Mike's life he was seriously considering becoming a Christian. 'On Tuesday,' he went on, 'we meet as directors; Mike should have been there. We will have an empty chair representing him during that day. But the next time we meet we will not have an empty chair, because we know that life invites us to go on.' He then invited us to close the service in an informal, student-like way: linking hands and singing 'He is Lord — He is Lord! He is risen from the dead and He is Lord! Every knee shall bow, every tongue confess, that Jesus Christ is Lord.' It was a moving moment to conclude a great service.

The reception afterwards was a replica of that on the funeral day. A host of people — academics, students, friends — all pressing our hands, anxious to identify themselves with us in our grief. Students were there who'd been at Owen Sound; the parents of students still in hospital. A young couple came up with some photographs. They told me that they'd become friendly with Mike and Catherine at 'Parenting Classes' just before and after James was born. That was their only contact; but they'd come to this service, and had shown me photos of proud parents; themselves with Mike and Catherine and their respective offsprings. Not for the first time, I gulped down a lump in my throat.

Gradually people drifted away, until just the family and

a few friends were left. I was amazed to see that it was after 5pm. We needed to relax, to slacken the taut tension; and indeed to sort ourselves out. For now we were staying in Hamilton: Maggie and David with Catherine, while we were going to the home of one of the McMaster professors and his wife. David and Vivienne Humphreys came from Yorkshire, but he enjoyed his work as a chemistry professor in Hamilton. Keen Christians both, they had strongly supported Mike in his work and witness, and were involved with IVCF. We'd met them the previous summer at Mike's barbecue, and they'd had us to a meal at their house. At the funeral service David had said to me, 'Let us know if there's anything at all we can do — I really mean that! We'll do anything we can to help you.' A couple of days later I took him up on it. 'David,' I said on the phone, 'you offered to help us out. Is there any chance you could put Ann and me up for a couple of days or so? We're coming to Hamilton on Sunday but we'll need somewhere to stay from Sunday night till Wednesday morning. We'll spend most of the time with Catherine, but she's putting up Maggie and Dave, so we were wondering if we could stay with you?' He readily agreed but later admitted he wasn't looking forward to it. 'What do we talk about?' he'd asked his wife. 'What on earth do we say to them?' I guess she just smiled and told him to be natural and normal. In the event they were marvellous, and a great help and encouragement to us, seeing to our every need and comfort.

But it poses the question: How do you relate to people tragically bereaved? You can't greet them with the conventional 'How are you?' when you know they are in emotional turmoil. There's no place for jocularity or light-hearted banter. Should you talk about the loved one? Should you say nothing at all? Silence becomes heavy-laden, and usually increases the tension. Yet you know the person is oppressed by the heavy grey blanket of grief. So how do you establish a relationship?

The key thing is sensitivity: an acute awareness of the

other person's emotional shock and pain. You have to relate to them where *they* are, and try to put yourself in their shoes. So comments like 'Feeling any better?' or 'Getting over it now, are you?' — as if the person has merely had a bad bout of flu — are out, way out! A bereavement is an emotional amputation; over time the pain will diminish, but always a vital part of *you* is missing. It is foolish to pretend it isn't, or that it doesn't matter.

The opposite to sensitivity is insularity: deliberately cutting oneself off from the pain of bereavement, wrapping oneself around in one's own affairs and so not reaching out or reacting to the trauma of death. I once heard of a housekeeper at a boy's boarding-school who was informed by one of the pupils that a boy had died as the result of a games accident that afternoon. 'Oh!' was her instinctive reaction, 'that means one less pint of milk to order tomorrow.' One gasps at such thick-skinned insularity.

Sensitivity is vital in seeking to relate to a bereaved person. However, a relationship is a two-way process. As well as reaching out your hand, the other's hand has to be proffered as well; there has to be a response. The sensitivity begins with gauging the other's response. For grief affects us all differently, which makes it difficult to set down guide-lines. For ourselves we found two things helpful. First, not to be ashamed of tears, nor embarrassed by them. Tears are an essential emotional release, they're part of our humanity (robots or computers don't cry). In times of great stress and grief they are a natural outlet of emotion — in fact, it would be unnatural not to weep. Secondly, we wanted to talk about Mike, to keep his memory alive, to recollect his jokes and his japes — even to laugh while doing so. This may not be for everyone, but it was right for us.

As a small boy I remember reading about a king of England (one of the early Henrys), whose son was drowned at sea. The historian wrote that from that moment on the king was never seen to smile, nor ever spoke of his son again. So be it; we found that for us we took comfort in the opposite course.

The Humphreys were sensitivity personified; leaving us alone when we wanted to be, chatting naturally when we needed company. Vivienne especially became our chauffeur, taking us hither and thither as and when we needed.

On Monday morning she dropped us off at Catherine's house, and while Ann and Maggie looked after James and the household chores, David and I accompanied Catherine into town to see about business affairs. The first stop was the bank; could Catherine pay bills on Michael's account now that he was deceased? This was too much for the teller at the counter so the manager was called; a dapper, grey-suited young man, hair smarted down, bristling efficiency. At first he played it by the book: a deceased person's account must be frozen for estate purposes. There is no estate, explained Catherine, there's a mortgage to be paid, and bills to be met. Eventually he relented, and opened an account in her name into which she paid in our church's cheque and others she'd been given; she could draw on this until the estate was cleared. It was a tiresome business, and though compassion gradually won the day, it could have been a lot easier.

The car insurance, which was in Michael's name, was much harder. This was conducted on the phone. 'My husband died in an accident ten days ago,' began Catherine. 'Right,' came the reply, 'we'll put you through to Claims.' But Claims didn't want to know, and put her through to Registration. 'My husband died in an accident ten days ago,' she tried again. 'Name?' 'Michael John Hare.' 'Yes, we have it here. We'll delete it then.' That's all, just delete his name, just as if Michael John Hare has been deleted from humanity, rubbed out, obliterated. We didn't phone in order to have his name deleted, but to have the insurance transferred to his brave, grieving widow. *Is there no place for sensitivity in business? Don't people matter as persons?* Maybe it's that some people can't cope with death and its reality, and insulate themselves against it. Yet death needs to be faced as a fact of life — the ultimate fact of life — and it's far better if it's accepted as such, without pretence, but with compassion.

After the warm fellowship of the Sunday service, the cold indifference of the Monday business was depressing in the extreme. But we all cheered up in the evening when Vivienne Humphreys had all of us to a meal — Dave, Maggie and Catherine and even wee James in his carry-cot in the corner. The main topic of conversation was the next evening's weekly meeting of the IVCF students on campus. A staff worker from another campus had offered to speak, but that wasn't the point. The students were still stunned, their faith shaken as they tried the impossible task of mentally reconciling a loving God with an awful tragedy, of coming to terms with the death, maiming and injury of their fellow students, fellow-believers. It was going to be a difficult evening with the tension taut tight.

'I think I ought to go,' said Catherine simply, 'so I will.' We all looked at her, and wondered, and marvelled.

'Do you really think you ought to?' someone asked. 'Do you think you'll manage to handle it?'

'Yes,' she said decisively. 'I really want to go.'

'Then we'll come with you,' said Ann, equally firmly. 'Unless you'd prefer us not to, then we could stay at home and look after James.'

'I'd like to go,' said Dave.

'We'll all go,' said Catherine, 'and we'll take James with us; that would be good, and they'll like that!' So it was decided we'd all go, all six Hares, to identify with the student body in their shock, bewilderment and grief. The young people set off for home and we slept soundly for the first time in ten days.

The cold, dull, grey weather continued. We didn't hurry the next morning; there wasn't much to hurry for. So it was after ten o'clock when Vivienne drove us across to Catherine's home.

'Is this David's first visit to Canada?' she suddenly asked.

'Yes, it is,' we replied. After a pause she said, 'I don't suppose he's seen Niagara Falls then? Do you think he'd like to?' We assured her he would.

'Then I'll take him,' she offered. 'We can collect him and I'll take him on from here.'

I marvelled at such a generous heart. This woman had expected to return home in half and hour, but was now committing herself to a day's outing without going back home again.

David jumped at the opportunity, and I offered to go along with them, as company for each. It was a forty-to-fifty-mile drive, a good hour on a good road, but in bleak weather . . . . January is not the best month to view the Falls, especially as there was driving sleet falling. It was still an impressive sight, however, and Dave took some photos to impress his two sons. We had a good hot lunch in a totally deserted restaurant, drove down through picturesque country beside the Niagara River to Niagara-on-the-Lake, a quaint old-fashioned town firmly keeping itself in the thirties to become a tourist attraction. Then the journey home through the grey twilight day, arriving back just in time to prepare for the IVCF meeting at 6.30pm.

We were warmly welcomed and invited to say a few words. I encouraged the students to stand firm in the faith, but David was able to identify more easily with them and spoke from his heart, underlining that, despite appearances, God is good and is in control and was alongside us in our grief and suffering. Andrew Lee gave us an update on the students still in hospital, and prayer was offered for them. Wisely the meeting was kept brief, and informal discussion, prayer and fellowship in small groups was encouraged. There were probably forty people there, out of the usual sixty; but these were unusual times. James, of course, was the centre of attention, though fast asleep in his carrycot. We were impressed with the warm friendliness and genuine sincerity of these young people, and thanked God for them.

I lay awake for a while that night — our last in Canada. I cried again at the thought of a blighted life, so full of promise. Then came the Scripture into my mind: ''"Unless an ear of wheat falls to the ground and dies, it remains only a single seed. But if it dies, it produces many seeds."'' As I meditated on those words, a 'word' came to me from God telling me that I must speak at the memorial service in England next month, and telling me exactly what I must say.

We packed our bags on Wednesday and said warm farewells to David and Vivienne. The youngsters looked bleary-eyed when we arrived. They explained that after the meeting Catherine had decided to go through all Mike's personal effects, his clothes, his desk, his books, and it had taken them half the night. She couldn't leave everything just as it was; she had to face the reality of her great loss. It was painful for them, but she and Maggie in particular released their stifled emotions, especially their anger, by doing so. They were angry at the event that had claimed two lives so full of promise, and had scarred — physically, emotionally and mentally — another eight youngsters. They were angry that this had happened at all, and to such a bright, up-coming man, one whom they each just happened to love dearly (as wife and as sister), one who was more than a close relation but their own particular best friend.

So together in their angry grief they cleared out Mike's belongings; Catherine couldn't bear to have Mike's 'things' but not have *him*. In addition, she wanted people who knew and loved Mike to have his things, knowing they'd appreciate them. She wanted each of us to have a recent material token of remembrance of Mike. David, of similar size and build, had some of his clothes and books. I accepted a couple of sweaters and some tapes. Altogether they'd filled a couple of suitcases for us to take back. These we would have to add to our luggage as we returned home. George came to collect us in his large car soon after lunch, but first we had an appointment with Don Posterski at the IVCF head office in Toronto.

We had asked for this meeting to try to sort out Mike and Catherine's personal affairs in the light of his death; it's frustratingly difficult to do this at a distance from a foreign land. He informed us that IVCF had insurance cover for all their employees, and that there was a double indemnity if the employee died while on IVCF business; and a Bible training weekend was 'normal business' for their staff workers. So we reckoned this would go a long way to paying off Catherine's huge mortgage which was not covered by a life insurance. She would also receive 'Workman's compensation' from the State as her husband had died at work in the course of his duties. We were relieved to hear all this, and that there was an Educational Trust Fund for James as well as a Welfare Fund for Catherine. He promised us that IVCF lawyers would handle the legal side of things as far as possible, and would put Catherine in touch with financial advisors. We could leave Canada assured that all was being done to take the strain of financial and legal matters off Catherine's back.

Don looked tired and drawn as he drove us to the McColl's house. What a week and a half you've had, I thought. If we are drained, you must be even more so — and then it told. Driving down the twelve-lane highway cutting through north Toronto, chatting about the accident and all its after-effects, Don suddenly put into words what we'd all thought but dare not say:

'C'mon, God,' he cried out, 'couldn't You take care of a snow-drift?' He glanced at us with a grim smile, and shook his head uncomprehendingly.

It raises, of course, the ultimate question, Could God have intervened? The difficulty for the Christian is that if you say 'Yes' then you ask, 'Well, why didn't He?', and He becomes a God who is either asleep or lazy or callous or indifferent — not at all the God of the Bible. But if you say 'No' then at once you say that He's not 'Almighty' God, that He is in fact powerless, weak, and not in control. How on earth (literally — we might understand in heaven!) do you reconcile this?

One answer is to say that He created a perfect world, but because of man's sin and rebellion the whole natural order is awry — hence earthquakes, hurricanes, and such-like natural disasters; and then to say that God doesn't tamper with His natural laws, doesn't intervene in any way. However, the next logical step is to say that He doesn't intervene at all in life, which is quite inconsistent with Jesus' teaching of an active God who guides and directs His children whenever they ask Him. And if we say He doesn't intervene in life, what is the point of prayer? Yet Jesus prayed, and He taught and urged us to pray. The Bible teaches that 'the prayer of a righteous man is powerful and effective'. (James 5:16.) That is, it affects much, it changes things! Tennyson was right: 'More things are wrought by prayer than this world dreams of' — it is the daily experience of millions!

So what about the prayer that affects nothing, that doesn't appear to affect things at all? The Christian can and must find his answer in the cross of Christ, for there we have the ultimate paradox: a holy God branded as a common criminal; an all-powerful God hanging helpless on a wooden gibbet; a creator God murdered by His own creatures; the paradoxes are extreme. Yet hold them together we must, or else we deny Him who died there. It is also true to say that if 'the fullness of God' dwelt in Jesus, he could have stepped down from the cross — as He was taunted to do — and very many would have believed as a result. When He was arrested, Jesus told Peter, who wanted to fight with a sword, ' "Do you think I cannot call on my Father, and he will at once put at my disposal more than twelve legions of angels?" ' (Matt. 26:53.) God could have intervened and God would have intervened, but Jesus knew that the cross was an essential part of God's plan for the salvation of all mankind.

So we are left with an all-powerful God who is willing to be vulnerable, whose very vulnerability is His strength. Out of that willingness to be vulnerable, which led to the crucifixion, there rose up the resurrection. For this resurrection not only vindicates Jesus but brings the blessed hope of new life to all who die in faith down the ages. The terror of the cross, when man murdered God, results in the glory of the resurrection, where God revitalizes man. The cycle of death and new life we see in nature is transposed to a cosmic scale.

So could God have taken care of that snow-drift? Of course He could, or He'd not be an almighty God. But He is also an all-vulnerable God, who takes upon Himself our weaknesses and thus limits Himself. And in our world He has no favourites: His rain falls on the just and on the unjust. Each and every one of us is prone to the vagaries of life, to its changes and chances, its accidents and its coincidences. By accepting this fairly obvious fact we are still affirming an all-powerful, all-loving, all-knowing — yet vulnerable — God. It's not the whole answer — we will never get there in this world — but it is part way towards one.

At the McColl's house we met the others and prepared for our overnight flight back to England. George drove us to the airport with Catherine, while Joan stayed at home to look after James. We drove in silence; this had been the longest week in our lives, a totally unreal week, quite unrelated to our normal daily life, yet a week during which we had faced the ultimate reality of life. We were glad it would soon be over.

The baggage was checked through without extra charge, and the awkward time for farewells came. Catherine told us how much she was looking forward to coming to Maggie's wedding in four months' time; and George told us that he had a business trip in Europe in May, and might be able to arrange to be there too. But the pain broke through the pleasantries, and we found ourselves crying on each other's shoulders.

'Catherine,' I choked through my tears, 'you are part of our family; you bear our name, and we'll always consider you one of us. We will pray for you and for James every day for the rest of our lives.' And I hugged her to me.

It was time to go: and perhaps like removing plaster from a wound, parting is best done quickly, with a sudden sharp pain, rather than long and drawn out, extending the anguish.

As we sat on the tarmac and gazed out of the plane, everything seemed unreal again — had it all been a dreadful nightmare — would we wake up in England and find it hadn't happened? Surely life-loving Mike would smile at us once more, in the land of the living, and we'd be chuckling again at his quips and antics. Was it really true that we'd consigned him to the ground, confined him to a grave? In our hearts we knew it was only too true, only too real, and the awful ache overwhelmed us.

The flight home was long and drawn-out. We dozed fitfully, fearfully, reflecting on the past extraordinary week, and anxious about the readjustment to the present reality of day-to-day living. Eventually we landed at Gatwick at 9am — an eight-hour flight, plus five hours time difference added on since leaving Toronto at 8pm.

Carolyn and her two boys were there to greet us on our arrival, and to take Dave home. It was a happy reunion, with the little lads zooming around, arms outstretched being aeroplanes, and they helped us to relax our tension and our tiredness.

One needs to realize that grief itself is tiring, exhausting. The encouragements to keep going, to live in the present, to occupy yourself, to accept that life must go on, are all valid; but life is also a burden and grief can't be shrugged off. It takes its toll, and drains the nervous energy. So food and sleep, the great restoratives, are essential. Yet these are the two things that grief often attacks. 'I don't feel like eating' is a common symptom of grief; yet one must. 'To sleep, perchance to dream, ay, there's the rub!' mused Hamlet. For the unconscious might take over, the night-thoughts howl through the head. Or sleep may be elusive, and the pillow become a sponge for tears. Grief will have its say, and grief will take its toll.

We had two weeks to prepare for the memorial service in Margate. At this service there would be our own family and friends; Mike's friends from student days; and our church family. So we wanted the service to relate to each group, if possible to involve people from those groups. We decided to ask Mike's closest friend and best man, Andrew Spear, now an Anglican clergyman, to give his reflections, and another close friend from Durham days, John Cook, also ordained, to lead the prayers; both responded positively. Two members of our congregation would read messages from Canada, while Colin would introduce the service and lead as needed. David agreed to read the lesson, and Maggie offered to play her flute accompanying the curate and his wife as they sang 'The Servant King'.

We decided to ask a long-standing friend, Alan Walker, a colleague from Uganda days where Michael was born, to give a meditation; and I insisted on speaking. Some weren't so sure about this, but I knew I had to, and I knew what God had given me to say. That left Ann. Could we involve her at all? It would be a powerful witness if the grieving mother could stand up front as well.

One of the letters of condolence which we had received contained a poem written by a member of our congregation. It was very poignant, brief, yet deep:

> 'He was my son
> And he was . . .
> Someone's husband,
> Somebody's friend,
> A brother to another,
> A father to his son.
> And in the tidal wave
> of grief

Deep calls unto deep
And a voice cuts through
The echoes in my mind . . .
"He was My son too;
He was My son too."'

Tentatively I asked Ann if she felt she could read it out at the service. She hesitated, and then affirmed: 'Yes, I'll do it. The Lord will have to strengthen me, but with His strength I'll do it!' That meant all four of us would take an up-front part, showing that grief need not be introspective, can be out-going and out-giving.

We left early for the church, as Ann and I had consciously decided that we would stand at the entrance door to greet people as they arrived — and arrive they did, from far and near. By the time the service was due to begin I looked around and for the third time in a month gasped at the large turn-out: again a full church with almost four hundred present.

We'd had printed a service sheet similar to the two in Canada, yet with a more winsome photo of Mike on the front. We used hymns that had been sung in Toronto and Hamilton: 'Praise to the Lord', 'He is Lord', and 'We trust in You'. David read the same passage from John's gospel that had been used in Hamilton: '"Unless an ear of wheat fall to the ground and dies it remains only a single seed. But if it dies, it produces many seeds."' It seemed so right. Ann read the poem so bravely and poignantly that many found it most moving. Another significant part was a very touching tribute to Mike that was sent to us signed by seventy staff, students or colleagues at McMaster University.

The meditation by our friend Alan Walker was — like the Christian faith itself — both simple and profound, and was centred on the Scripture passage which David had just read. It was an inspired and inspiring message.

My own talk I'd entitled 'Questions to consider', because I knew that everyone present was asking 'Why? Where is

God?' 'Couldn't God look after His own?' I knew it was better to face these questions head on. So I said:

'This tragic event — a young man active in the Lord's service suddenly cut off in the prime of life — raises all sorts of questions. But there is one it's not even worth asking: the question "Why?" Don't ask "Why did God allow it to happen?" because you'll get no satisfactory answer, and you'll drive yourself mad if you allow it to dominate your thinking. There is no adequate answer in this life, and so it's useless to try to find one. Even Jesus asked "Why?" on the cross: "My God, my God, Why . . . " — and the only answer was a long, dark, heavy silence. The only safe approach — safe because sane — is indicated by two cards we were sent: the first said simply, "Dear God, I don't understand You but I do trust you". The second, a hand-written script by a middle-aged widow, read: "We don't know why, but we do know why we trust God, who knows why." And that's the best place to leave that question.

'But there are other questions, probably unspoken, which those of little or no faith ask themselves; those whose faith is shaky — and shaken by events like this; the questions of doubters and waverers, and unbelievers — and the first question — in the light of this tragic loss — is very probably: "Where is your God now?" "Where is God in all this?" And I want to affirm: He is right here. God has never been closer to us — and I speak for Maggie and Dave, for Ann and for Catherine, too. He's been sharing in our agony and anguish, sharing in our tears and in our grief. How do I know?

'First, the Scriptures tell us that Jesus wept when His great friend Lazarus died. Jesus also says, "You are my friends, if you obey my commandments." Mike was a friend of Jesus, for he was doing Jesus' will; and Jesus wept when Mike died, wept with us. God is grieving with us today because God Himself knows what it's like to have a son killed in the prime of manhood. God is with us because He's within us.

'But He's also outside us: He's our Support, our Comforter — in the true sense of "Strengthener". He's our Enabler, and we are carried by His loving care. Where is our God? He's right here, with us and around us, supporting, sustaining, enabling.

'All right, the doubter may say, your God is with you in this. But why couldn't He look after His own? This is a harder question, but let's look at it this way. Suppose the Prime Minister made his wife the Foreign Secretary, his son the Home Secretary, and placed his nephews and nieces in positions of power and authority. Even his most ardent supporters would probably despise him for that! We dislike a leader who abuses his power by showing favouritism to his own family. It sometimes happens in "banana republics", and our reaction is one of scorn and contempt. And so with God. If there's a disaster — a railway station engulfed with fire, say — and a hundred people doomed to die, but eight are miraculously plucked out by God because they are practising Christians — is that God looking after His own? Do we really want a God who "looks after His own" like that, but lets the other ninety-two go hang? I would feel bitter and angry at such a callous God, whose only concern was with those who acknowledged Him, and who had no interest whatsoever in anyone else.

'God sends His rain on the just and on the unjust alike; He doesn't play favourites; and if He did, of course, there'd be thousands jumping on the Christian bandwagon as an insurance policy to save their own skins, instead of the real and only reason: to love and serve and worship Him.

'Finally, our doubter may ask, what possible good can come out of this tragic accident? Again, the answer is not in this life, not fully. However, there are certain pointers: In this church, the body of Christ has become a much greater and deeper reality: when one suffers, all suffer, has been truly reflected here. We are more aware of identifying with each other in Christ now, and the response of this church — both in practical terms and in pastoral concern —

has been enormous. Great good is already happening among us.

'The Christians in Toronto and Hamilton, too, have been brought face-to-face with death, and through it their faith has been strengthened, their priorities altered. The day after the funeral the IVCF office in Toronto received a letter saying that Mike's death had made the writer — a student — seriously consider the claims of Christ to commit her life to Him. There will be fruit from the death of this seed, of that we can be sure. After all, the greatest tragedy in the world occurred on Good Friday, when men murdered God. But the greatest triumph came from that event — the resurrection.

'This sad event confronts us, too, doesn't it? It makes us all ask, Am I ready to meet my Maker? Is it not time I came to terms with God, and gave Him the allegiance of my heart, life and service? After all, He is the God who strengthens us in our sorrows. He is the God who is within us weeping and outside us enabling; He is the God who does not play favourites; and He is the God who — supremely on the cross — brings triumph out of tragedy. He is the God whom Mike loved and served.'

At the end of the service there was again a 'reception' with tea and cakes provided by willing helpers of our church. Again we were amazed at people's response to our bereavement and to Mike's memory; some had travelled from Bath, some from Birmingham, others from Reading and Cambridge — all to be with us for an hour's memorial service. Friends from student days, friends from school days — all came to pay their respects. I reckoned that even allowing for overlap, well over a thousand people attended the three services held for Michael — a marvellous tribute to a young man of just 27 years of age.

How well do parents know their children? We'd always thought of Mike as being just like us; very ordinary, well-meaning, God-fearing, law-abiding people. It was emerging that he was, in fact, somewhat exceptional. We know full well that being 'ordinary' does not mean being boring, dull and mediocre — Mike the joker had certainly learnt that. But he was not only 'a great all-round chap to have around', as a person he was obviously a good few degrees above average.

This was confirmed to us when we were graciously asked by Carleton University in Ottawa, where Mike did his post-graduate research for two and a half years, if they could endow a Memorial Fellowship for post-graduates to his memory and bearing his name. (This was the contents of the envelope handed to us at the funeral service in Toronto by the Scottish geography professor.) It seemed to be his 'approachableness' that endeared him to so many. The citation read, 'It is *Mike Hare the person* that we at Carleton, like many others, remember most. His enduring characteristics of caring, compassion, humaneness, and good humour were a source of inspiration, comfort and joy to those who had the privilege of knowing him. So it is to try to reflect something of these human, personal characteristics that the annual award is granted on the basis of academic achievement, combined with a particular con-tribution to the quality of working relationships among students in the department, or between students and staff.' There can't be many student fellowships where 'the quality of working relationships' is a major factor in the award. We were delighted — and humbled.

Mike's motto, his exhortation to his students, was 'Keep an Eternal Perspective' and we took it upon ourselves to encourage others to do likewise. So when we were ten-tatively asked if we'd be willing to be interviewed for an article in our parish news-sheet, to go into 5,000 homes at Easter, we readily agreed. It was written as a question and answer item, and when Ann was asked 'Did you struggle with the question, "Why us?"' she replied: 'No, that was not a struggle. The question that we did struggle with was, "Why any young person?" — and there is no real answer. We don't ask why. We don't know why. We know that we trust the God who does know why. God seemed to be saying that all those young students whose lives Mike had touched for God can take the Word of God further than Mike could ever have gone!'

'How do you cope with the sadness?'

'It's hard, but there's also a sense of victory and peace, a feeling that he is not gone forever!'

'What do you mean, "not gone forever"?'

'The body is only a shell, a carton. His carton is empty, finished with, but Mike lives on. Not just in our memories, but in the spiritual lives of the students he worked among.'

I was able to end with an affirmation of the Easter message; death is not the end, because Christ rose again. Through the darkness of Good Friday we have the joy of Easter Sunday. As we link our life with Jesus we are linked on to the resurrection-life, the eternal perspective.

Two years and nine months after Mike died there was a Student Mission at McMaster University. It had been arranged three years earlier by Mike himself, who'd booked the experienced evangelist. The leader of the Christian Union was one of the men who had been in the accident at Owen Sound and his leadership was strong, genuine and positive. The Mission was a blessing to many, and Catherine was able to attend some sessions. For us it set the seal of God on Mike's work.

We have heard that the Christian Union at McMaster, forty strong when Mike started, eighty when he died two years later, now numbers — a further five years on — 400 members. A monthly Sunday evening worship service is regularly drawing 500-600 people. Death can — does — lead to resurrection!

For ourselves, we are greatly encouraged and give praise to God as we continue to see fruit springing up from the fallen seed, and to realize that many are finding — as Mike wished, worked, prayed, and lived for — an 'eternal perspective' to their lives.

EPILOGUE

Coming to terms with Loss

Coping with the death of a loved one, especially a young person, poses all sorts of problems. It affects our whole being — emotionally, intellectually, spiritually — and drains us of energy. Downcast and listless, we try to cope, to continue with life as best we can, yet grief pervades us, overwhelms us, and has to be accommodated into our life. Because we are complex human beings we react in different ways.

Some years ago a couple who were friends of ours lost their youngest daughter at the age of 11, through what should have been a routine operation. The parents reacted in opposite ways. Her father coped by absorbing himself in his work (which was demanding) and never speaking about his daughter at all; her mother wanted to share about her, talk about her, reminisce and remember. So she visited us, saying, 'You're the only people I can talk to about my daughter; John won't even listen.' We try to cope in different ways, and yet there are false comforters about still, as in Job's day; our attitude — towards God, to life and death — is all important, and a positive attitude will best help us as we become acquainted with grief.

Let us first make the distinction between death and grief. Death is nearly always an unwelcome visitor: sometimes suddenly pouncing, hawk-like, out of the blue; sometimes anticipated, even expected; occasionally longed for, to put an end to pain, suffering, dementia. Whenever he comes he brings hurt; and he's always accompanied by his awful accomplice, grief. Leering, stalking grief, death's dark shadow, dogs our weary feet, hangs around us and over us, and casts a gloomy spell upon our blighted lives. So how do we handle him?

There are stages of grief; initially the shock, the numbness, the unreality of it all. Then the reality sinks in, the loss is raw and painful as the numbness wears off, and we find ourselves howling. Frustration and anger surface too, and it's important to remember that it's natural to cry, it's natural to be angry. The third stage is an aimless apathy, a withdrawal from social gatherings because 'they don't understand'. It's often a depressing no-man's-land when well-meaning comforters ask pointless questions. At each stage a strong ingredient of the cure it to recognize that this is normal, that you are swimming with the stream in a river called grief. You are not going mad, despite your forgetfulness, your lack of concentration, your loss of appetite; it is all part of the process called grief.

How we handle these stages of grief — which are not necessarily sequential but weave in and out of our lives in fits and starts — depends a good deal upon our attitude. In particular grief will force upon us the great mysteries: Is there a God out there who loves me, and if so why does He take my loved one from me? Is death itself the end, or is there life beyond the grave? Is God responsible for the death of my loved one, and is my beloved now with God? These are profound questions which we ignore or thrust away while we are enjoying life together, but which we are forced to consider when a loved one dies. Even when we're moving towards an answer we're still left with a mystery.

I recently read of a small boy of 11 who knew he was dying. When his sister asked him if he felt afraid he replied, 'Not really; I think it's going to be rather exciting, like looking into a mirror and discovering where you've come from!' His attitude was so right. He recognized, with penetrating insight, that 'our end is our beginning' as T. S. Eliot wrote — so much more refreshing than the doleful funeral chant: 'dust to dust, ashes to ashes'.

The body does shrivel and shrink, wither and die. If we can realize that this is the outward shell, the casing for the inner 'me', we'll be greatly helped.

Death, of course, is the taboo subject in our culture, the one topic that is not talked about. Perhaps in a society that has lost most of its belief in a loving, personal God, we dare not mention death because of fear. There's an impenetrable mystery around it.

Grief still hangs around, of course, and we still react to

it. Some it shocks into depressive passivity; others try to shake it off by frenetic activity. Still it hangs about: some days oppressive, on top of one; other days distant, subdued in a dark corner, yet sullenly making its presence felt. Once while driving to work about a month after Mike had died I was thinking affectionately and longingly about him. Something welled up inside me, and I shouted at the top of my voice — '27 is too young to die! 27 is too young to die!' — the words of the minister at Mike's funeral service. Somehow I felt better for venting my grief on the morning air. A few weeks later, when grief was sitting heavily on my shoulders, I reversed my car in an empty car park — straight into the side of an unseen stationary vehicle. My awareness was more of grief than of motoring.

Generally we didn't find introspective books on grief particularly helpful. As Christians we found the best antidote was to contemplate the cross, and to rejoice in the resurrection with the positive, assured, confident hope that it brings. We need to look beyond the grave to the glory of Heaven. As Ingrid Trobisch, in her sensitive and telling book *Learning to Live Alone* (IVP, London, 1986) writes: 'The hole is still there. Somehow my Lord is the One who enables me to live with that hole. He hasn't filled it up yet, but He has made a bridge over it. I can live with it now, and I can stand on the bridge as I reach out to others.'

In coping with our own grief, our understanding of God is all-important. If we regard God as harsh and vindictive, or as uncaring and unconcerned, we'll only go on hurting ourselves as we shake our fist at Heaven.

Death is a part of life, and we need to accept that fact. Christians assert also that God not only knows all about it, but has experienced it. We affirm that there is a God who does actually care about us — not just collectively, but personally and individually cares about *me!* We look to Christ, who reveals God to us, and we see God in action, and just how much He loves us. Jesus Christ knows, from first-hand experience, the excruciating agony of prolonged torture, and the intense suffering of a lingering death. God knows what it is like to lose a son in His prime, and I can take comfort from this. He's not an uncaring God; He can and does identify both with those who suffer and with those who grieve. He's been there!

All He asks is that we acknowledge Him, accept Him, and then He comes to us, gently giving an inner peace and strength and comfort that nothing can destroy. Gradually the hole begins to be bridged, and His consoling love enables us to live with the loss.

So our attitude to God, our awareness of Him and of His ways and purposes is significantly important when it comes to any consideration of death. Here there are two extremes to avoid, and a simple central way to follow. The first extreme is fatalism: 'It is the will of God' — that is, the incomprehensible will of an inscrutable and indifferent Deity, whose plaything is man. We can't affect what happens, so anything that does happen is 'the will of God'. Thus we should accept this stoically. God is impenetrable, His ways past knowing, so we accept fatalistically whatever happens — and that includes death. This way there is little solace or comfort.

The second extreme leads almost to the same end, but by an opposite route. It is an attitude that believes that God is so in control of our lives (or certainly a believer's life) that nothing untoward can ever happen; that everything that happens is completely controlled by God, including death and apparent 'accidents'. We've been given books to read, supposedly to help us, written by Christian parents who'd lost a child tragically. But they made me angry, for I felt their theology was awry. The argument goes something like this: 'Our child's usefulness to God on earth was done, so God took him to Himself' — maybe via a car crash, maybe a mountaineering accident, whatever. It reflects the pagan philosophy: 'Those whom the gods love die young.' The point is that God had decided at that moment He would pluck the beloved child from his family to be with Him —

usually by an accident or disease. One such book actually had the sentence: 'There are no accidents with God.' In other words He directly causes everything to happen. No accidents! What about the Fall of Man, for a start? Was that accident or design? For much of our understanding of death stems from the Fall of Man. I believe that God 'allows' accidents, 'allows' death, but in no way is the cause of them, nor responsible for them.

I believe that Mike's death was an accident, and not a part of God's design or plan. I cannot believe otherwise, or else the God I worship would be guilty of taking another life at the same time as Mike's, physically injuring four others and mentally scarring nine students. I don't believe 'Mike's usefulness to God on earth was finished'; that's a large part of the tragedy! I even shy away from the phrase 'the Lord has called him to Himself' as it still makes God the responsible agent. Ann and I firmly believe that Mike died as the result of an accident, that God was no way accountable for his death (even if He knew the accident would happen).

So where was God in this accident? Asleep? Impotent?

I've been helped in thinking through this problem by an observation in Philip Yancey's *Disappointed with God*. So many of us, he says, confuse 'God' with 'life'. That is well worth pondering. 'Life' is patently unfair from the moment of birth. The blessings are distributed very unevenly indeed. It's a minority of babies who are born with all the advantages; the majority inherit at least one of the disadvantages: poor health; poverty; maladjustment; physical or mental handicap; uncaring parents; inadequate facilities; unhappy home life; and so on. Then when we sometimes get 'stung', or when our day or our car fails to run smoothly, we spread out our hands and say, 'That's life' — yes, that is life, but it's not God, who is loving and caring all the time. In life accidents happen, disease strikes, calamities occur; often, it seems, these things happen randomly, to whom they will. A Christian friend who herself had lost a daughter, once said to us, 'The Lord has given my brother-in-law the great privilege of suffering with "M.E.".' This I could not accept, but was too much of a coward to say so. This is a random shot from life; it's not the Lord's doing. Neither was Mike's accident, nor David's. This I believe is affirmed by the Bible, our touchstone of truth.

In the Sermon on the Mount, Jesus teaches that God, 'sends his rain on the just and on the unjust'. Expanded, this spells out that the 'righteous' don't have any special privileges, that they are as subject to the changes and chances of this life as the next man. This is surely borne out by history and by experience. However, it's an age-old puzzle: 'Why do the wicked flourish?' cried the Psalmist, observing that the righteous often suffer. It is because God has no favourites, and believing in Him is not an insurance policy against disaster or tragedy. The Christian believer is as much prone to the ups and downs of life, the 'slings and arrows of outrageous fortune', as the unbeliever. So why be a Christian, what's the point if it makes no difference? Simply because it makes all the difference! 'When I walk through the valley of the shadow of death — *Thou art with me.*' God is with the believer in his suffering, in his sadness, in his sorrow. And the knowledge of that is not only comforting but positively strengthening. There is also the assurance that God is there, sharing in the suffering, consoling in the desolation, and giving hope in the future.

The cross is the focus of this, and makes it all real. God actually does share in the sufferings of mankind, bearing his spiritual burdens as well as experiencing the physical agony. It's a revelation of the height and depth of God's love, that He endured this for us. Indeed, there are few deprivations of human life that Jesus did not experience: a refugee — homeless — misunderstood by parents — hungry — physically abused — single — lied about — beaten up — unjustly accused — unfairly punished — mocked and jeered at — forsaken by close friends — betrayed by a colleague —

He knows about them all, He's been there! Life did not flow smoothly for the Son of God.

The cross also is a victory sign: that goodness does and can triumph over evil. For out of the degradation of the crucifixion came the victory of the resurrection. And good can and often does come out of the unmitigated disasters (which is *NOT* to say that God 'caused' the disaster so that good could emerge, nor that the eventual good 'justifies' the terrible tragedy). Mike's death has in fact resulted directly in some finding faith in Christ, including one girl involved in the accident who experienced the love and comfort of caring Christians, and saw how faith helped others. It has resulted in a booming ministry at McMaster University, and while this is not *why* God let it happen, He has brought good out of evil, hope out of the loss.

The sceptic may still be unconvinced; Paul recognized that to the wise the cross was foolishness. But the 'foolishness' of God is far wiser than the wisdom of man, and the best answer to this paradox is that offered by former Archbishop William Temple:

'"There cannot be a God of love," men say, "because if there were, and He looked upon the world, He'd do something about it." The Christian points to Jesus, and says, "He did." "God made the world," men say, "so He is responsible for all the suffering, and He should bear the load." The Christian points to the cross and says, "He did!"'

It is worth looking at the three occasions mentioned in the gospels when Jesus confronted death, two of whose victims were youngsters. The daughter of Jairus, the synagogue ruler, was but 12 years old when she died of a sickness. (Luke 8:41, 42, 49-56); Jesus restored her to life. The coffin of a deceased young man was being carried to the burial ground outside the town of Nain when Jesus came upon it. His heart went out to the widow, whose only son this was, and He restored the young man to life. (Luke 7:11-15.) In neither case did He tell the grieving parents,

'This is the will of God,' or 'Your child's usefulness to God on earth has finished.' Nor did He tell them stoically to accept what had happened, and to face it out bravely. Indeed, if God had 'called to Himself' these two children as part of His plan and purpose for them, then Jesus would have been acting contrary to God's will in restoring them to life; and that would be unthinkable. Jesus accepted it as a tragedy in both cases, a tragedy of life, and in His loving compassion did something about it — as much as anything for the sake of the grieving parents. Significantly, each of these episodes were recorded by Luke, who was both a Gentile and a medical doctor.

The most detailed account of Jesus dealing with death occurs in John's gospel, chapter 11, where He hears that His friend Lazarus has died. And we learn that 'Jesus wept.' (Verse 35.) Again, Jesus is not accepting Lazarus' early death as 'God's will'. True, He says 'it is for God's glory, so that God's Son may be glorified through it' by restoring him to life. But nowhere did He say or imply it was God's will for Lazarus to die, and if He believed it was, he could not possibly have gone against that will by raising him from the dead.

Tragedies happen — it's part of the human condition. And it's no use blaming God, or trying to rationalize the tragedy as part of God's will. It needs to be accepted as part of the mystery of the suffering of humanity — which itself is a result of the 'Fall of Man'.

'Acceptance' and 'mystery' are two concepts the human mind does not take to easily. We want to question acceptance, to penetrate the mystery — and rightly so: this is the way of progress, of extending the frontiers of knowledge, of understanding. But there is a limit. And by definition the finite will never fathom *fully* the Infinite, the mortal will never *fully* understand the Immortal, the creature never comprehend *fully* the Creator. There is still a mystery at the heart of it all, and we need to accept this mystery which lies at the very core of life, of death, of suffering, and of God. For me this acceptance in no way diminishes an all-loving and all-powerful Creator God.

'All-powerful?' That raises huge questions. If He really is all-powerful why does He allow so much human suffering, so much tragedy, and on such a large scale? Why doesn't He intervene? The only honest answer I know is, 'I don't know!' He is the Creator, I'm the creature. I don't know, but He does, and I trust Him because I've known something of the great love He has for me. It's a hard lesson for rational man to accept, but accept it we must.

An American Rabbi lost his son in mid-adolescence from a terrible aging disease, so that at fifteen natural years he had aged to seventy. The Rabbi wrote a book about it, *When Bad Things Happen to Good People*, in which he tried to come to terms with this same conundrum: what's an all-loving and all-powerful God doing when bad things happen to good people. (He didn't, incidentally, try to define 'good', which in Christian terms includes absolutely no one.) He took us through the book of Job — the right starting place for any in-depth view of suffering — but ended with a fairly impotent God, almost unable to cope with all the sin and suffering. But Job should provide the end as well as the beginning. After all the arguments, doubts, and questionings, the Lord answers Job:

> ' "Who is this that darkens my counsel
>   with words without knowledge?
> Brace yourself like a man;
> I will question you,
> and you shall answer me.
> Where were you when I laid the earth's
>   foundation?
> Tell me, if you understand.
> Who marked off its dimensions?
> Surely you know!" '
> (Job 38:2-4.)

Of course the creature cannot understand the Creator —

they are of different orders of creation! No more could a beetle or a butterfly 'understand' man. So the Lord challenges Job:

> '"Will the one who contends with the Almighty
>   correct him?
> Let him who accuses God answer him!"' (40:2.)

To his credit Job acknowledges his lowliness:

> '"I am unworthy — how can I reply to you?
> I put my hand over my mouth.
> I spoke once, but I have no answer —
> twice, but I will say no more."' (40:4, 5.)

God continues to question Job even more deeply:

> '"Would you discredit my justice?
> Would you condemn me to justify yourself?"'
> (40:8.)

and piles question upon question regarding His creative power in nature. Then Job replied to the Lord:

> '"I know that you can do all things;
> no plan of yours can be thwarted.
> You asked, 'Who is this that obscures my
> counsel without knowledge?'
> Surely I spoke of things I did not understand,
> things too wonderful for me to know."'
> (Job 24:2, 3.)

And there the book of Job ends — almost. Job, who had suffered disaster upon disaster, and had argued and questioned and deliberated and debated with three unhelpful 'comforters', finally realizes that 'God is God'. Moreover, God loves him, and shows that Job is special to Him by blessing him abundantly — 'The Lord blessed the latter part of Job's life more than the first' (42:18). At the heart of all suffering, and of God Himself, is a profound mystery.

We have found that when bad things happen we are cast more than ever upon a God of love who makes His presence very real, who draws very close to us. We find that questioning gets nowhere, and leads only to mental turmoil; but trusting brings swiftly that 'peace that passes all understanding' — and that is what we need the most at such times (if not all the time). Faith is one of those attributes which, like love, increases the more you use it; the more you share it, exercise it, or give it away, the more it grows. Faith flowers into a peace that resides at the very core of our being, firm and unshakeable.

So the great conundrum of an all-loving, *and* an all-powerful God, who allows bad things and accidents to happen, is yet another of the great paradoxes of Christianity. And like the other paradoxes — the Divine becoming human, the Immortal put to death, the omnipresent confined to space and time — we have to assert both truths and hold them in tension. These paradoxes come together and are pin-pointed at the cross.

For the Christian the mystery of suffering can only be viewed in the light of the cross — an empty cross — for Christ's crucifixion and resurrection are of one piece: they go together, as each is meaningless without the other. The Oxford theologian Alister McGrath affirms straightforwardly: 'The cross and resurrection may be said to mark the dawn of a new era in the history of the world. Socrates may have shown us how to die with dignity; Jesus Christ shows us how to die in hope.' And He goes on to show us how the cross liberates us from the fear of death, a fear of which many are secret prisoners: 'It allows us to face death with a quiet and calm confidence, knowing that its sting has been drawn by the cross, and victory given through the resurrection.'

God is all-love, and all-caring; and the love of God, shown supremely on the cross, is all-powerful. It can break the power of drug addiction, transform bitterness and resentment into forgiveness, change lives for the better, as countless books testify. God is also sovereign, and all-knowing. Jesus affirms this: '"Are not two sparrows sold for a penny? Yet not one of them will fall to the ground apart from the will of your Father . . . . So don't be afraid; you are worth more than many sparrows.''' (Matt. 10:29-31.) God is aware of their falling, but He doesn't knock them to the ground! The fatal falling is a part of life; the caring concern is a part of God. The Christian asserts both the power of God and the love of God and, though it may stretch him, holds them together.

In the face of death or disaster, then, as we become acquainted with grief, how should we react? First, recognize that God knows, God cares; God is with us in this tragedy, and He understands — the cross is proof of that. Secondly, realize that it is an empty cross that is the centre of our faith, symbolizing the sure and certain resurrection hope. Christianity teaches that death is not the end, that there is a hope beyond the grave, so that the Apostle Paul is able to say: 'I reckon that the sufferings we now endure bear no comparison with the glory, as yet unrevealed, which is in store for us.'

Humanly speaking, also, we need to recognize that death is a part of life, that we are all born to die. There's no reason at all for it to be a taboo subject, to be kept under wraps, hushed up, or talked about only in soft tones, as if it is improper to mention it at all. Of course grief and sorrow sit heavily on our shoulders, and their attendants, guilt and remorse, are never far away. But why do we dress it up so, and lay it on so thick: sombre black clothes and all the funereal trappings? Grief must be expressed, but it must be genuine and real and true. Reality and truth are found in the heart, not in the outer garments. The comfort of God is found in the heart, too, once that heart is open to Him.

A realization that death has been defeated by Christ's cross is a source of great comfort and strength. It's still with us, of course, but its ultimate defeat is assured: 'The last enemy that shall be conquered is death.' Death itself is doomed to die!

So we need to 'keep an eternal perspective' — in a God

who knows, who has experienced death, who loves passionately and cares compassionately about His creatures, who acknowledges the tragedies in life, yet who is Sovereign Lord. As we become acquainted with grief, so we become acquainted with the suffering Son of God, and in our sorrow and sadness can say with the Apostle Paul: 'Praise be to the God and Father of our Lord Jesus Christ, the Father of compassion and the God of all comfort, who comforts us in all our troubles . . . . For just as the sufferings of Christ flow over into our lives, so also through Christ our comfort overflows.' (2 Cor. 1:3-5.) To God be the glory!